math
expressions
Common Core

Dr. Karen C. Fuson

 Watch the frog come alive in its pond as you discover and solve math challenges.
Download the *Math Worlds AR* app available on Android or iOS devices.

Grade 1
Volume 1

 This material is based upon work supported by the
National Science Foundation
under Grant Numbers
ESI-9816320, REC-9806020, and RED-935373.

Any opinions, findings, and conclusions, or recommendations expressed in this material
are those of the author and do not necessarily reflect the views of the National Science Foundation.

Unit 2 | Addition and Subtraction Strategies

© Houghton Mifflin Harcourt Publishing Company

BIG IDEA 3 - Mixed Story Problems

BIG IDEA 3 - Addition Strategies

Student Resources

Dear Family:

Your child is learning math in an innovative program that interweaves abstract mathematical concepts with the everyday experiences of children. This helps children to understand math better.

In this program, your child will learn math and have fun by

- working with objects and making drawings of math situations
- working with other children and sharing problem-solving strategies with them
- writing and solving problems and connecting math to daily life
- helping classmates learn

Your child will have homework almost every day. He or she needs a **Homework Helper.** The helper may be anyone—you, an older brother or sister (or other family member), a neighbor, or a friend. Make a specific time for homework and provide your child with a quiet place to work (for example, no TV). Encourage your child to talk about what is happening in math class.

In Lessons 1 and 2, your child will learn to see numbers as a group of 5 and extra ones. Making mental pictures by grouping units in this way will later help your child add and subtract quickly. Children benefit greatly from learning to "see" numbers without counting every unit.

✂ -

Please fill out the following and return it to the teacher.

My child _____ will have _____ as his or her
            (child's name)   (Homework Helper's name)

Homework Helper. This person is my child's _____.
                                      (relationship to child)

CC SS **Unit 1 addresses the following standards from the** Common Core State Standards for Mathematics: **1.OA.A.1, 1.OA.B.3, 1.OA.C.5, 1.OA.C.6, 1.OA.D.8, and all** Mathematical Practices.

Children start exploring these 5-groups by looking at dots arranged in a row of 5 plus some extra ones. Below are samples that show the numbers from 6 through 10.

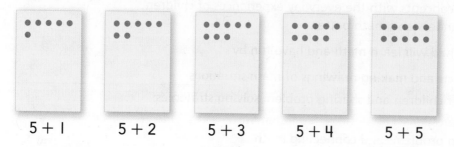

| 5 + 1 | 5 + 2 | 5 + 3 | 5 + 4 | 5 + 5 |

The teacher gives the children a number and asks them to say it as a 5 plus extra ones. Children say the numbers in order at first. Later they can "see" the quantities even when the numbers are shown randomly.

On some homework pages, you will find instructions that ask children to "see the 5." Your child is being encouraged to make a mental picture of a number that contains a 5-group. Later, the children will be asked to see groups of 10 by combining two 5-groups. This will help them learn place value.

It takes repeated exposure to such groups for children to see the numbers quickly. Many of the visual aids in your child's classroom include 5-groups. Children tend to absorb these visual patterns without realizing it.

If you have any questions or if your child is having problems with math, please contact me.

Sincerely,
Your child's teacher

Estimada familia:

Su niño está aprendiendo matemáticas con un programa innovador que relaciona conceptos matemáticos abstractos con la experiencia diaria de los niños. Esto ayuda a los niños a entender mejor las matemáticas.

Con este programa, su niño aprenderá matemáticas y se divertirá mientras:

- trabaja con objetos y hace dibujos de problemas matemáticos;
- trabaja con otros niños y comparte estrategias para resolver problemas;
- escribe y resuelve problemas y relaciona las matemáticas con la vida diaria;
- ayuda a sus compañeros a aprender.

Su niño tendrá tarea casi todos los días y necesita a una persona que lo ayude con la tarea. Esa persona puede ser usted, un hermano mayor (u otro familiar), un vecino o un amigo. Establezca una hora para la tarea y ofrezca a su niño un lugar tranquilo donde trabajar (por ejemplo un lugar sin TV). Anime a su niño a comentar lo que está aprendiendo en la clase de matemáticas.

En las Lecciones 1 y 2, su niño aprenderá a ver los números como un grupo de 5 más otras unidades. El hecho de agrupar mentalmente unidades de esa manera ayudará a su niño a sumar y restar rápidamente en el futuro. Los niños se benefician muchísimo de aprender a "ver" los números sin contar cada unidad.

Por favor complete la siguiente información y devuelva este formulario al maestro.

La persona que ayudará a mi niño _____ es
(nombre del niño)

_____ . Esta persona es _____ de mi niño.
(nombre de la persona)   (relación con el niño)

CC SS **En la Unidad 1 se aplican los siguientes estándares de los** Estándares estatales comunes de matemáticas: **1.OA.A.1, 1.OA.B.3, 1.OA.C.5, 1.OA.C.6, 1.OA.D.8 y todos los de** Prácticas matemáticas.

Los niños comienzan a practicar con estos grupos de 5 observando puntos distribuidos en una fila de 5 más otras unidades. Estos ejemplos muestran los números del 6 al 10.

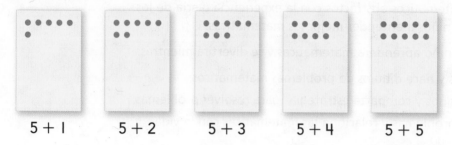

5 + 1   5 + 2   5 + 3   5 + 4   5 + 5

El maestro les da un número a los niños y les pide que lo digan como 5 más otras unidades. Al principio, los niños dicen los números en orden. Más adelante pueden "ver" las cantidades incluso cuando los números se muestran sin un orden específico.

En algunas páginas de tarea hallará instrucciones que piden a los niños "ver el número 5". A su niño se le está animando a que visualice un número que contenga un grupo de 5. Más adelante, se les pedirá que vean grupos de 10, combinando dos grupos de 5. Esto les ayudará a aprender el valor posicional.

Es necesario que los niños practiquen muchas veces los grupos de este tipo para que puedan llegar a ver los números rápidamente. Muchas de las ayudas visuales que hay en el salón de clase incluyen grupos de 5. Los niños tienden a absorber estos patrones visuales sin darse cuenta.

Si tiene alguna pregunta o algún comentario, por favor comuníquese conmigo.

Atentamente,
El maestro de su niño

doubles

pattern

4 + 4 = 8
Both partners are the same.
They are **doubles**.

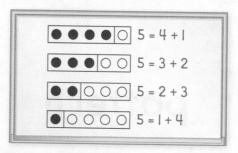

The partners of a number
show a **pattern**.

Cut on dashed lines.
Do not cut on solid lines.

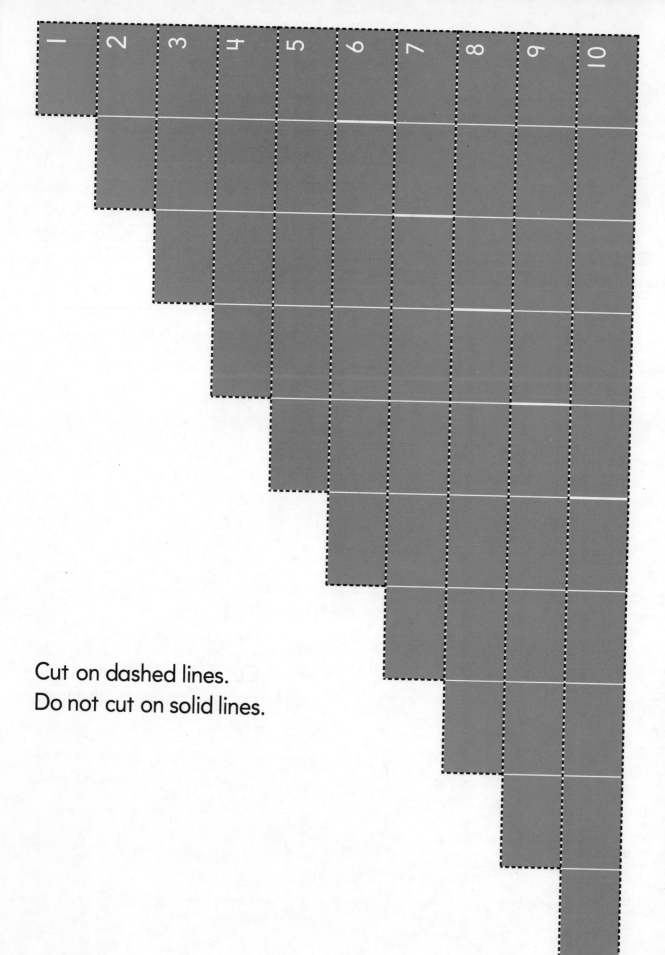

Cut on dashed lines.
Do not cut on solid lines.

Stair Steps

Write how many dots.

1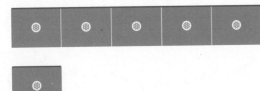

1 and 1 more is _____.

2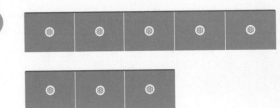

3 and 1 more is _____.

3

5 and 1 more is _____.

4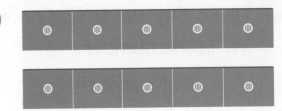

5 and 3 more is _____.

5

5 and 4 more is _____.

6

5 and 5 more is _____.

7   5 crows in a row
and 4 below.
How many crows?

_____ crows

5 in a row

4 below

Solve.

8 Chen says 5 and 4 more is 7.

Help Chen find the error.

Draw to explain.

5 and 4 more is ☐.

9 Use a 5-group to find how many.
Write the numbers.

_____ and 3 more is _____.

Draw to explain.

 Check Understanding

Explain how to use Stair Steps to show 6 as a
5-group and extra ones.

6	1
7	2
8	3
9	4
10	5

Number Cards 1–10

Name _____

Circle the 5-group. Write how many dots.

1. ☐

2. ☐

3. ☐

4. ☐

5. ☐

6. ☐

7. **Draw a line to match the dots to 5 plus extra ones.**

• 5 + 1

• 5 + 3

• 5 + 4

• 5 + 2

• 5 + 5

CC SS Content Standards **1.OA.A.1, 1.OA.C.5**
Mathematical Practices **MP7, MP8**

8 Draw a 5-group and extra ones to show 6.

9 Draw a 5-group and extra ones to show 9.

10 Create a story for 7. Draw a 5-group and extra ones to show your story.

_____

_____

_____

_____

✓ **Check Understanding**
Show numbers 6 through 10 as 5-groups and extra ones.

Visualize Numbers as a 5-Group and Ones

See the 5-group.
Draw extra dots to show the number.

1 8

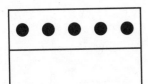

2 10

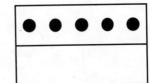

Write how many dots.
See the 5 in each group.

3

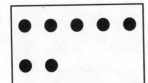 ☐

4

 ☐

5

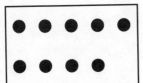 ☐

Name _____   Date _____

1 Show 9 with a 5-group and extra ones.

2 Use words or pictures to tell a story about your groupings.

Dear Family:

Your child is learning to find the smaller numbers that are "hiding" inside a larger number. He or she will be participating in activities that will help him or her master addition, subtraction, and equation building.

To make the concepts clear, this program uses some special vocabulary and materials that we would like to share. Below are two important terms that your child is learning:

- **Partners:** Partners are two numbers that can be put together to make a larger number. For example, 2 and 5 are partners that go together to make the number 7.

- **Break Apart:** Children can "break apart" a larger number to form two smaller numbers. Your child is using objects and drawings to explore ways of "breaking apart" numbers of ten or less.

Partners of 7

Children can discover the break-aparts of a number with circle drawings. They first draw the "Break-Apart Stick" and then color the circles to show the different partners, as shown below. Sometimes they also write the partners on a special partner train, which is also shown below.

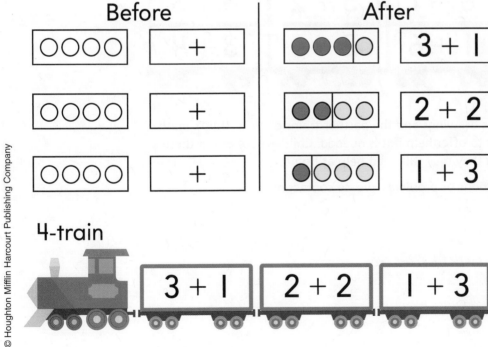

Later, children will discover that partners can change places without changing the total. This concept is called "switch the partners." Once children understand switching partners, they can find the break-aparts of a number more quickly. They simply switch each pair of partners as they discover them.

Shown below are the break-aparts and switched partners of the number 7. Sometimes children also write this information on a double-decker train.

Break-Aparts of 7

 | 6 + 1 | or | 1 + 6

 | 5 + 2 | or | 2 + 5

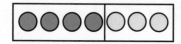 | 4 + 3 | or | 3 + 4

Double-Decker Train

7-train

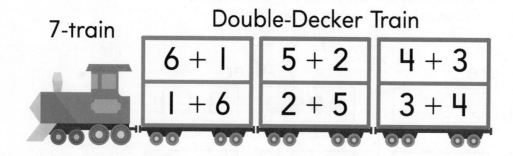

| 6 + 1 | 5 + 2 | 4 + 3 |
| 1 + 6 | 2 + 5 | 3 + 4 |

You will see the circle drawings and the partner trains on your child's math homework. Be ready to offer help if it is needed. Children are doing these activities in class, but they may still need help at home.

If you have any questions or problems, please contact me.

Sincerely,
Your child's teacher

CC SS **Unit 1 addresses the following standards from the** Common Core State Standards for Mathematics: **1.OA.A.1, 1.OA.B.3, 1.OA.C.5, 1.OA.C.6, 1.OA.D.8, and all** Mathematical Practices.

Estimada familia:

Su niño está aprendiendo a hallar los números más pequeños que están "escondidos" dentro de un número más grande. Va a participar en actividades que le ayudarán a dominar la suma, la resta y la formación de ecuaciones.

Para clarificar los conceptos, este programa usa un vocabulario especial y algunos materiales que nos gustaría mostrarle. A continuación hay dos términos importantes que su niño está aprendiendo:

- **Partes:** Partes son dos números que se pueden unir para formar un número más grande. Por ejemplo, 2 y 5 son partes que se unen para formar el número 7.

- **Separar:** Los niños pueden "separar" un número más grande para formar dos números más pequeños. Su niño está usando objetos y dibujos para explorar maneras de "separar" números iguales o menores que diez.

Partes de 7

Los niños pueden separar un número usando dibujos de círculos. Primero dibujan un "palito de separación" y luego colorean los círculos para indicar las partes, como se muestra a continuación. A veces los niños anotan las partes en un tren de partes especial, que también se muestra a continuación.

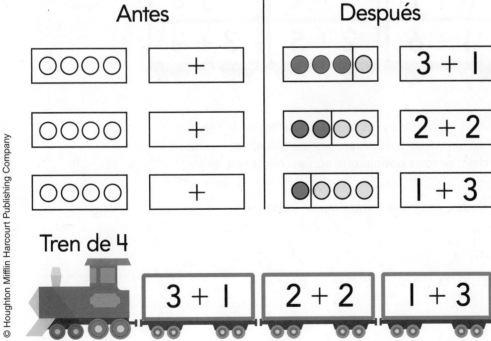

© Houghton Mifflin Harcourt Publishing Company

Luego, los niños van a aprender que las partes pueden intercambiar su posición sin que varíe el total. Este concepto se llama "cambiar el orden de las partes". Una vez que los niños entienden el cambio del orden de las partes, pueden encontrar las partes de un número con más rapidez. Sencillamente cambian cada par de partes a medida que las encuentran.

A continuación están las partes, y las partes en otro orden, del número 7. A veces los niños escriben esta información en un tren de dos pisos.

Partes de 7

 | $6 + 1$ | y | $1 + 6$

 | $5 + 2$ | y | $2 + 5$

 | $4 + 3$ | y | $3 + 4$

Tren de dos pisos

Tren de 7

| $6 + 1$ | $5 + 2$ | $4 + 3$ |
| $1 + 6$ | $2 + 5$ | $3 + 4$ |

Usted verá los dibujos de los círculos y los trenes de partes en la tarea de matemáticas de su niño. Ayúdelo, si es necesario. Los niños están haciendo estas actividades en clase, pero es posible que aún así necesiten ayuda en casa.

Si tiene preguntas o dudas, por favor comuníquese conmigo.

Atentamente,
El maestro de su niño

En la Unidad 1 se aplican los siguientes estándares de los Estándares estatales comunes de matemáticas: **1.OA.A.1, 1.OA.B.3, 1.OA.C.5, 1.OA.C.6, 1.OA.D.8 y todos los de** Prácticas matemáticas.

Write the partners.

1 ●●●●|○ $5 = 4 + 1$

●●●|○○ $5 =$ _____

●●|○○○ $5 =$ _____

●|○○○○ $5 =$ _____

2 ○○○|○ $4 = 3 + 1$

○○|○○ $4 =$ _____

○|○○○ $4 =$ _____

3 ●●|○ $3 = 2 + 1$

●|○○ $3 =$ _____

4 ●|○ $2 =$ _____

5

5 ∧ □ □   5 ∧ □ □   5 ∧ □ □   5 ∧ □ □

6

4 ∧ □ □   4 ∧ □ □   4 ∧ □ □

Use **patterns** to solve.

VOCABULARY
patterns

7 $2 + 0 = \boxed{}$ $5 + 0 = \boxed{}$ $3 + 0 = \boxed{}$

    $4 + 0 = \boxed{}$ $1 + 0 = \boxed{}$ $0 + 3 = \boxed{}$

    $0 + 5 = \boxed{}$ $0 + 2 = \boxed{}$ $0 + 4 = \boxed{}$

8 $4 + 1 = \boxed{}$ $2 + 1 = \boxed{}$ $3 + 1 = \boxed{}$

    $1 + 1 = \boxed{}$ $1 + 4 = \boxed{}$ $1 + 3 = \boxed{}$

9 $2 + 2 = \boxed{}$ $3 + 2 = \boxed{}$ $1 + 2 = \boxed{}$

10 $2 - 0 = \boxed{}$ $4 - 1 = \boxed{}$ $3 - 2 = \boxed{}$

✓ **Check Understanding**

Make circle drawings for all the partners of 5.

1 Show and write the 6-partners.

◯◯◯◯◯◯   ___ + ___   6 = _____

◯◯◯◯◯◯   ___ + ___   6 = _____

◯◯◯◯◯◯   ___ + ___   6 = _____

◯◯◯◯◯◯   ___ + ___   6 = _____

◯◯◯◯◯◯   ___ + ___   6 = _____

2 Write the 6-partners.

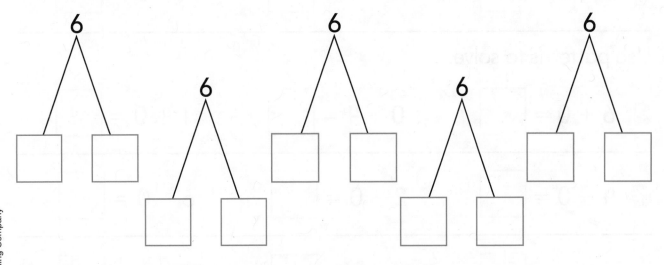

3 Write the 6-partners as a train.

6-train

[+] [+] [+] [+] [+]

CC SS Content Standards **1.OA.B.3, 1.OA.C.5, 1.OA.C.6, 1.OA.D.8**
Mathematical Practices **MP1, MP2, MP6, MP7, MP8**

4 Discuss patterns in the partners.

VOCABULARY
doubles

2	**3**	**4**	**5**	**6**
1 + 1	2 + 1	3 + 1	4 + 1	5 + 1
		2 + 2	3 + 2	4 + 2
				3 + 3

Use **doubles** to solve.

5 3 + 3 = ☐   1 + 1 = ☐   2 + 2 = ☐

6 − 3 = ☐   2 − 1 = ☐   4 − 2 = ☐

Use patterns to solve.

6 6 + 0 = ☐   0 + 4 = ☐   1 + 0 = ☐

7 4 − 0 = ☐   2 − 0 = ☐   6 − 0 = ☐

8 3 − 3 = ☐   5 − 5 = ☐   1 − 1 = ☐

4 − 4 = ☐   2 − 2 = ☐   6 − 6 = ☐

✓ **Check Understanding**

Write all the partners of 6.

___ + ___ , ___ + ___ , ___ + ___ , ___ + ___ , ___ + ___

Partners of 6

Name _____

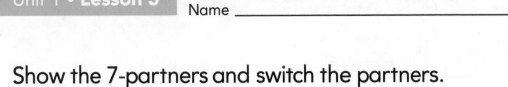

Show the 7-partners and switch the partners.

1 ⬜ ○○○○○○○   _____ + _____   and   _____ + _____

2 ⬜ ○○○○○○○   _____ + _____   and   _____ + _____

3 ⬜ ○○○○○○○   _____ + _____   and   _____ + _____

Write the partners and the switched partners.

4 7-train

5

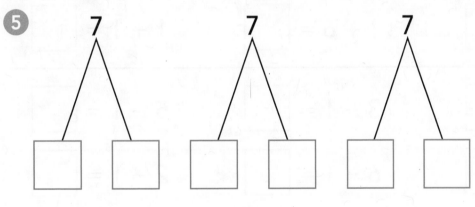

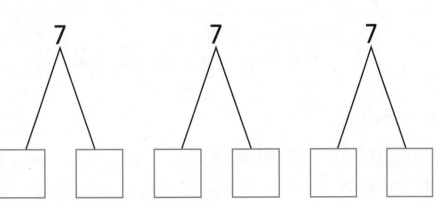

6 Discuss patterns in the partners.

2	**3**	**4**	**5**	**6**	**7**
1 + 1	2 + 1	3 + 1	4 + 1	5 + 1	6 + 1
		2 + 2	3 + 2	4 + 2	5 + 2
				3 + 3	4 + 3

Use patterns to solve.

7 $3 + 1 = \square$ $6 + 1 = \square$ $4 + 1 = \square$

$5 + 1 = \square$ $2 + 1 = \square$ $1 + 1 = \square$

8 $1 + 2 = \square$ $1 + 5 = \square$ $1 + 4 = \square$

$1 + 3 = \square$ $1 + 6 = \square$ $1 + 1 = \square$

9 $7 - 1 = \square$ $3 - 1 = \square$ $5 - 1 = \square$

$4 - 1 = \square$ $6 - 1 = \square$ $2 - 1 = \square$

10 $5 - 4 = \square$ $7 - 6 = \square$ $3 - 2 = \square$

✓ **Check Understanding**

Explain the pattern you see when you switch the partners for 7.

Name _____

Show the 8-partners and switch the partners.

1. ⃝⃝⃝⃝⃝⃝⃝⃝   ___ + ___   and   ___ + ___

2. ⃝⃝⃝⃝⃝⃝⃝⃝   ___ + ___   and   ___ + ___

3. ⃝⃝⃝⃝⃝⃝⃝⃝   ___ + ___   and   ___ + ___

4. ⃝⃝⃝⃝⃝⃝⃝⃝   ___ + ___   and   ___ + ___

Write the partners and the switched partners.

5. 8-train

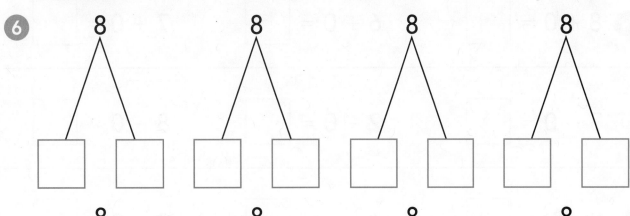

6.

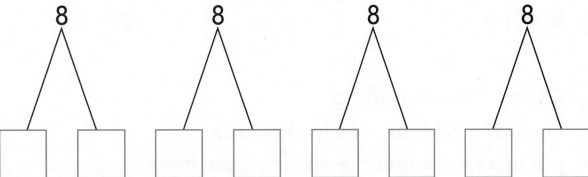

© Houghton Mifflin Harcourt Publishing Company

CC SS Content Standards **1.OA.B.3, 1.OA.C.6, 1.OA.D.8**
Mathematical Practices **MP1, MP2, MP7, MP8**

7 Discuss patterns in the partners.

2	3	4	5	6	7	8
1 + 1	2 + 1	3 + 1	4 + 1	5 + 1	6 + 1	7 + 1
		2 + 2	3 + 2	4 + 2	5 + 2	6 + 2
				3 + 3	4 + 3	5 + 3
						4 + 4

Use doubles to solve.

8 $4 + 4 = \square$ $\qquad$ $3 + 3 = \square$ $\qquad$ $2 + 2 = \square$

$8 - 4 = \square$ $\qquad$ $6 - 3 = \square$ $\qquad$ $4 - 2 = \square$

Use patterns to solve.

9 $8 + 0 = \square$ $\qquad$ $6 + 0 = \square$ $\qquad$ $7 + 0 = \square$

10 $7 - 0 = \square$ $\qquad$ $2 - 0 = \square$ $\qquad$ $8 - 0 = \square$

11 $4 - 4 = \square$ $\qquad$ $6 - 6 = \square$ $\qquad$ $2 - 2 = \square$

✔ **Check Understanding**
Draw Math Mountains to show the partners for 8 and the switched partners.

$\qquad$ Partners of 8

Show the 9-partners and switch the partners.

1 OOOOOOOOO   _____ +   and   _____ +

2 OOOOOOOOO   _____ +   and   _____ +

3 OOOOOOOOO   _____ +   and   _____ +

4 OOOOOOOOO   _____ +   and   _____ +

Write the partners and the switched partners.

5 9-train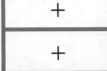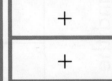

6

9   9   9   9

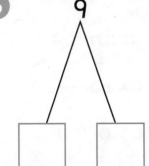 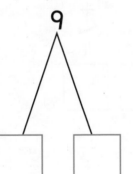 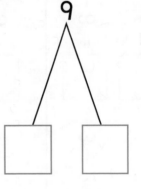 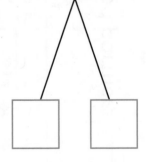

9   9   9   9

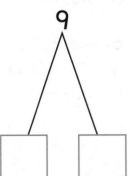 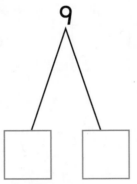 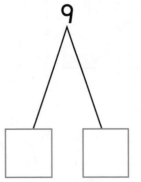 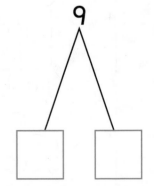

7 Discuss patterns in the partners.

2	3	4	5	6	7	8	9
1 + 1	2 + 1	3 + 1	4 + 1	5 + 1	6 + 1	7 + 1	8 + 1
	2 + 2	3 + 2	4 + 2	5 + 2	6 + 2	7 + 2	
		3 + 3	4 + 3	5 + 3	6 + 3	7 + 3	
			4 + 4	5 + 4	6 + 4		

Use patterns to solve.

8 6 + 1 = ☐   8 + 1 = ☐

4 + 1 = ☐   3 + 1 = ☐

9 1 + 7 = ☐   1 + 2 = ☐

1 + 8 = ☐   1 + 4 = ☐

10 9 − 1 = ☐   3 − 1 = ☐

7 − 1 = ☐   6 − 1 = ☐

11 9 − 8 = ☐   3 − 2 = ☐

7 − 6 = ☐   6 − 5 = ☐

✔ **Check Understanding**

Write all the partners of 9 and the switched partners.

___ + ___ , ___ + ___ , ___ + ___ , ___ + ___ ,

___ + ___ , ___ + ___ , ___ + ___ , ___ + ___ ,

1 Discuss patterns.

Partners of 10

9 + 1	8 + 2	7 + 3	6 + 4	5 + 5
1 + 9	2 + 8	3 + 7	4 + 6	

Write the 10-partners.

2

10 = 9 + 1

10 = 8 + 2

10 = _____

10 = _____

10 = _____

10 = _____

10 = _____

10 = _____

10 = _____

3

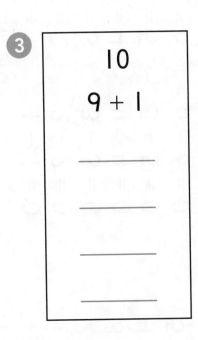

10

9 + 1

_____

_____

_____

_____

CC SS Content Standards **1.OA.B.3, 1.OA.C.6, 1.OA.D.8**
Mathematical Practices **MP1, MP2, MP6, MP7, MP8**

4 Discuss patterns.

Patterns with Partners

2	3	4	5	6	7	8	9	10
1 + 1	2 + 1	3 + 1	4 + 1	5 + 1	6 + 1	7 + 1	8 + 1	9 + 1
		2 + 2	3 + 2	4 + 2	5 + 2	6 + 2	7 + 2	8 + 2
				3 + 3	4 + 3	5 + 3	6 + 3	7 + 3
						4 + 4	5 + 4	6 + 4
								5 + 5

Patterns with Zero

1 + 0 = 1	1 − 0 = 1	1 − 1 = 0
2 + 0 = 2	2 − 0 = 2	2 − 2 = 0
3 + 0 = 3	3 − 0 = 3	3 − 3 = 0
4 + 0 = 4	4 − 0 = 4	4 − 4 = 0
5 + 0 = 5	5 − 0 = 5	5 − 5 = 0
6 + 0 = 6	6 − 0 = 6	6 − 6 = 0
7 + 0 = 7	7 − 0 = 7	7 − 7 = 0
8 + 0 = 8	8 − 0 = 8	8 − 8 = 0
9 + 0 = 9	9 − 0 = 9	9 − 9 = 0
10 + 0 = 10	10 − 0 = 10	10 − 10 = 0

Patterns with Doubles

1 + 1 = 2
2 + 2 = 4
3 + 3 = 6
4 + 4 = 8
5 + 5 = 10

Check Understanding

Write the partners of 10 and the switched partners of 10.

Partners of 10

Name _____

Write the number of band members in each column or row.

1

____ ____ ____ ____ ____ ____ ____ ____

2

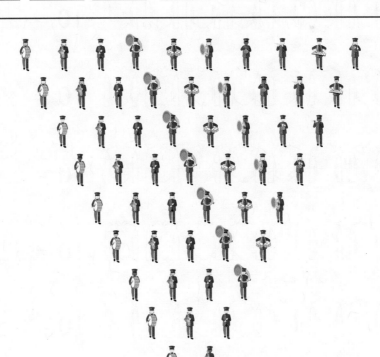

____
____
____
____
____
____
____
____
____
____

CCSS Content Standards 1.OA.B.3, 1.OA.C.5, 1.OA.C.6
Mathematical Practices MP1, MP4, MP5

3 Show and write the partners of 10.

10 = _____ + _____

10 = _____ + _____

10 = _____ + _____

10 = _____ + _____

10 = _____ + _____

10 = _____ + _____

10 = _____ + _____

10 = _____ + _____

10 = _____ + _____

Focus on Mathematical Practices

Name _____

Date _____

Write two more partners for the number.

1 6 ⬜⭕⭕⭕⭕⭕⭕

$6 = 5 + 1$

$6 =$ _____

$6 =$ _____

2 8 ⬜⭕⭕⭕⭕⭕⭕⭕⭕

$8 = 7 + 1$

$8 =$ _____

$8 =$ _____

Use doubles or patterns to solve.

3 $0 + 4 =$ ⬜

4 $4 + 4 =$ ⬜

5 $7 - 0 =$ ⬜

Name _____ Date _____

1 Write the partners.

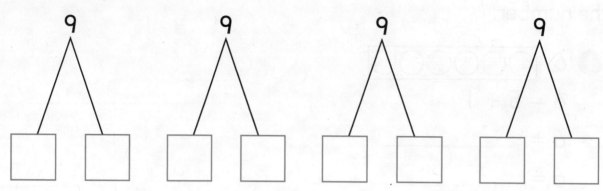

2 Choose a set of 9-partners. Write or draw a story about the 9-partners.

See the 5-group.
Draw extra dots to show the number.

1   **7**

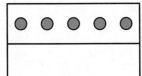

2   **8**

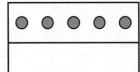

3 Does the picture match the number?
Choose Yes or No.

7

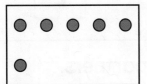

    ○ Yes   ○ No

8

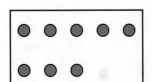

    ○ Yes   ○ No

5

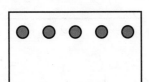

    ○ Yes   ○ No

4 Choose all the 10-partners.

- ○ 2 + 8
- ○ 3 + 5
- ○ 8 + 3
- ○ 8 + 2

---

5 Complete the 6-partners.

$6 = 5 +$ | 1 |
  | 2 |
  | 3 |

$6 = 4 +$ | 0 |
  | 1 |
  | 2 |

$6 =$ | 0 |
  | 1 | $+ 6$
  | 2 |

---

6 Write the numbers in the boxes to show the partners.

| 1 | 2 | 3 | 4 | 5 | 6 | 7 | 8 |

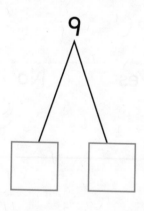
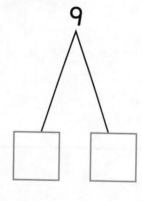
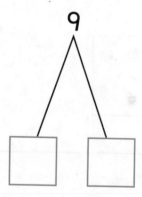

---

7 Use patterns to solve.

$6 + 1 =$ ☐ $5 + 1 =$ ☐ $4 + 1 =$ ☐

Write the partners.

8 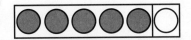 $5 = $ _____ + _____

9  $7 = $ _____ + _____

10  $6 = $ _____ + _____

11 Write facts that match each total.

| 8 + 1 | 9 + 0 | 6 + 1 | 4 + 4 | 7 + 0 | 1 + 7 |

7	8	9

Write the partners and the switched partners.

12   [___ + ___] and [___ + ___]

13   [___ + ___] and [___ + ___]

14 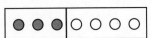   [___ + ___] and [___ + ___]

15 Use patterns to solve.

$3 - 1 = \boxed{}$

$4 - 1 = \boxed{}$

$5 - 1 = \boxed{}$

16 Draw a story about a set of 8-partners.
Write the partners.

Plant Flowers

1 Draw 5 flowers growing in the pot.
Make some red. Make some yellow.

2 Write the 5-partners the flowers show.
Then switch the partners.

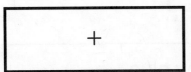

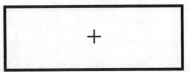

3 Draw 10 flowers growing in the pot.
Make some blue. Make some yellow.

4 Write the 10-partners the flowers show.
Then switch the partners.

5 Can you show 10 with blue and yellow flowers
in other ways? Tell why or why not.

_____

_____

Color Plates

6 Draw 9 plates. Make some red. Make some blue.

7 Write the 9-partners that the plates show.
Then switch the partners.

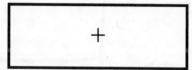   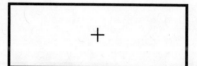

---

8 Color the plates below yellow. Then draw blue
plates to make 10 plates in all.

9 Write the 10-partners the plates show.
Then switch the partners.

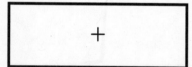   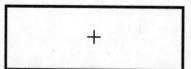

10 Can you show another number of blue plates to
add to the yellow plates to make 10 in all?
Tell why or why not.

_____

_____

Dear Family:

Your child has started a new unit on addition, subtraction, and equations. These concepts are introduced with stories that capture children's interest and help them to see adding and subtracting as real-life processes.

At the beginning of the unit, children show a story problem by drawing a picture of the objects. If they are adding 4 balloons and 2 balloons, for example, their pictures might look like the top one shown here. If they are subtracting, their pictures might look like the bottom one.

Addition

Subtraction

In a short time, children will show objects quickly with circles rather than pictures. This is a major conceptual advance because it requires the use of symbols. Children are asked to show the partners (4 + 2) as well as give the total (6). From here, children are just a small step away from writing standard equations, such as 4 + 2 = 6 and 6 − 4 = 2.

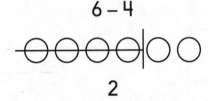

To keep them focused on the actual problem, children are often asked to give a "complete answer" in class. This means that they should name the objects as well as give the number. Right now, complete answers are not required for homework. Even so, it would be helpful for you to ask your child to say the complete answer when working with you at home. Example: "You said the answer is 6. Is it 6 dinosaurs? No? Then 6 what? . . . Oh! 6 balloons!"

Sincerely,
Your child's teacher

CC SS **Unit 2 addresses the following standards from the** Common Core State Standards for Mathematics: **1.OA.A.1, 1.OA.B.3, 1.OA.C.5, 1.OA.C.6, 1.OA.D.7, 1.OA.D.8, and all** Mathematical Practices.

Estimada familia:

Su niño ha empezado una nueva unidad sobre la suma, la resta y las ecuaciones. Estos conceptos se presentan con cuentos que captan el interés de los niños y les ayudan a ver la suma y la resta como procesos de la vida diaria.

Al comienzo de la unidad, los niños muestran un problema en forma de cuento haciendo un dibujo de los objetos. Por ejemplo, si están sumando 4 globos y 2 globos, sus dibujos pueden parecerse al dibujo de arriba. Si están restando, es posible que sus dibujos se parezcan al dibujo de abajo.

Suma

Al poco tiempo, los niños mostrarán objetos rápidamente con círculos en vez de dibujos. Esto es un gran paso conceptual, ya que requiere el uso de signos. A los niños se les pide que muestren las partes (4 + 2) y la respuesta (6). Una vez que hacen esto, están casi listos para escribir ecuaciones normales, tales como 4 + 2 = 6 y 6 − 4 = 2.

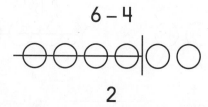

Resta

4 + 2

OOOO|OO

6

Problema de suma

6 – 4

OOOO|OO

2

Problema de resta

Para que sigan concentrándose en el problema mismo, a los niños se les pide una "respuesta completa" en la clase. Esto significa que deben nombrar los objetos y dar el número. Actualmente, no se requieren respuestas completas en la tarea. Sin embargo, sería de ayuda si le pidiera a su niño que le dé la respuesta completa cuando trabaja con Ud. en casa. Por ejemplo: "Dijiste que la respuesta es 6. ¿Son 6 dinosaurios? ¿No? Entonces, ¿6 de qué?. . . ¡Ajá! ¡6 globos!"

Atentamente,
El maestro de su niño

© Houghton Mifflin Harcourt Publishing Company

Represent Addition

count on

total

equation

vertical
form

subtract

$4 + 3 = 7$ $\begin{array}{r} 4 \\ +\ 3 \\ \hline 7 \end{array}$

total →

$5 + 4 = \boxed{9}$

$5 + \boxed{4} = 9$

$9 - 5 = \boxed{4}$

5 · · · ·
   6 7 8 9

Count on from 5 to get the answer.

$\begin{array}{r} 6 \\ +\ 3 \\ \hline 9 \end{array}$ $\begin{array}{r} 9 \\ -\ 3 \\ \hline 6 \end{array}$

$4 + 3 = 7$ $7 = 4 + 3$

$9 - 5 = 4$ $4 = 9 - 5$

$8 - 3 = 5$

Name _____

Write the partners and the total.

1 ☐ + ☐

✳✳✳✳✳ | ✳✳✳✳

Total ☐

2 ☐ + ☐

Total ☐

3 ☐ + ☐

⚽⚽ | ⚽⚽⚽⚽

Total ☐

4 ☐ + ☐

Total ☐

5 ☐ + ☐

Total ☐

6 ☐ + ☐

Total ☐

7 Draw a picture of flowers to
show 4 + 2. Write the total.

Write the partners and the total.

8 ☐ + ☐

Total ☐

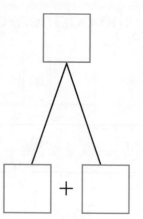

---

9 ☐ + ☐

Total ☐

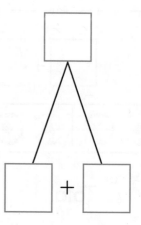

---

10 ☐ + ☐

Total ☐

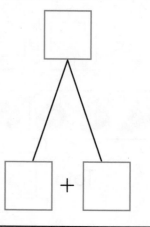

✓ Check Understanding

Listen to the math story. Then draw it and write the partners and the total.

Represent Addition

Write the partners and total for each circle drawing.

1 ☐ + ☐

⬤⬤⬤⬤⬤ ⬤｜◯◯

Total ☐

2 ☐ + ☐

⬤⬤⬤⬤⬤ ⬤⬤⬤｜◯◯

Total ☐

3 ☐ + ☐

⬤⬤⬤⬤⬤｜◯◯◯◯

Total ☐

4 ☐ + ☐

⬤⬤⬤⬤｜◯ ◯◯

Total ☐

5 ☐ + ☐

⬤⬤⬤⬤⬤ ⬤⬤｜◯◯◯

Total ☐

6 ☐ + ☐

⬤⬤⬤⬤｜◯ ◯

Total ☐

7 Make a circle drawing to show 5 + 5.

Match the pictures to the circle drawings.

 ⑧

☐ + ☐

● ● ● ● ● | ○ ○

Total ☐

⑨

☐ + ☐

● ● | ○ ○ ○ ○ ○ ○

Total ☐

⑩

☐ + ☐

● ● ● | ○ ○ ○ ○

Total ☐

✔ Check Understanding

Use the circle drawing to tell a math story. Explain how to use the circles to represent the story.

Addition with Circle Drawings

Name _____

Write the partners and the total. Then write the **equation**.

1  ☐ + ☐

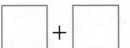

_____
Equation

Total ☐

2 ☐ + ☐

_____
Equation

Total ☐

3 ☐ + ☐

_____
Equation

Total ☐

4 ☐ + ☐

_____
Equation

Total ☐

5 Write an equation of your own. _____

Write the partners and the total. Then write the equation.

6  +

Total ☐

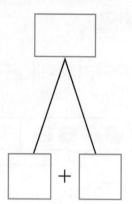

_____
Equation

7  +

Total ☐

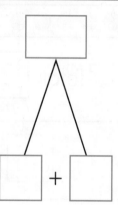

_____
Equation

© Houghton Mifflin Harcourt Publishing Company

 PATH to FLUENCY **Add.**

1 $1 + 0 =$ ☐   **2** $0 + 8 =$ ☐   **3** $6 + 0 =$ ☐

✓ **Check Understanding**

Write an equation with numbers on each side
of an equal sign. ____ + ____ = ____

Addition Equations

Name _____

Make a circle drawing for the story problem.
Write the equation.

1 There are 4 elephants drinking from the
river. Then 2 more elephants join them.
How many elephants are there in all?

_____
Equation

2 Teresa plants 5 roses in the garden. Hugo
plants 4 roses. How many roses did they
plant in all?

_____
Equation

3 Henry played 6 outside games last week.
Then he played 3 computer games. How
many games did he play altogether?

_____
Equation

Circle if the equation is true or false.

Draw a line to change $=$ to $\neq$ if it is false.

Draw to explain.

4 $2 + 3 = 3 + 2$

true   false

5 $6 + 1 = 5 + 1$

true   false

6 $4 + 4 = 7 + 2$

true   false

7 $3 + 2 = 1 + 4$

true   false

✓ **Check Understanding**

Complete the equation to make it true.

$3 + 4 = 5 + \boxed{}$

Addition Equations and Stories

Name _____   Date _____

Write the partners and the total.

 1   [   ] + [   ]    2   [   ] + [   ]

Total [   ]   Total [   ]

Write the partners and total.

3   [   ] + [   ]   4   [   ] + [   ]

Total [   ]   Total [   ]

Write a true equation for the story.

 5   7 plates are on the table.
Anna puts 3 more plates on the table.
How many plates are on the table now?

_____

Name _____   Date _____

Add.

1 2 + 0 = ☐   **2** 0 + 4 = ☐   **3** 7 + 0 = ☐

4 0 + 1 = ☐   **5** 3 + 0 = ☐   **6** 0 + 5 = ☐

7 9 + 0 = ☐   **8** 0 + 8 = ☐   **9** 6 + 0 = ☐

10 0 + 10 = ☐   **11** 5 + 0 = ☐   **12** 0 + 7 = ☐

13 8 + 0 = ☐   **14** 0 + 9 = ☐   **15** 10 + 0 = ☐

Dear Family:

Earlier in the unit, your child solved addition problems by making math drawings and counting every object. This is called *counting all*. Now your child is learning a faster strategy that allows them to work directly with numbers. The method they are learning is called *counting on*. It is explained below.

In an addition problem such as 5 + 4, children say (or "think") the first number as if they had already counted it. Then they count on from there. The last number they say is the total. Children can keep track by raising a finger or making a dot for each number as they count on. The diagram below shows both the finger method and the dot method.

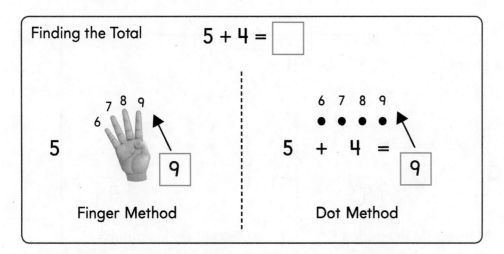

Counting on requires repeated practice. This is provided in class activities and homework assignments. Right now, your child is learning how to find unknown totals. In the next unit, he or she will learn to use the Counting On strategy to subtract.

Counting on is a temporary method to help children build fluency with addition and subtraction within 10. The goal by the end of the grade is for children to automatically know the answer when the total is 10 or less.

Sincerely,
Your child's teacher

Unit 2 addresses the following standards from the Common Core State Standards for Mathematics: **1.OA.A.1, 1.OA.B.3, 1.OA.C.5, 1.OA.C.6, 1.OA.D.7, 1.OA.D.8, and all** Mathematical Practices.

Estimada familia:

Un poco antes en la unidad su niño resolvió problemas de suma haciendo dibujos matemáticos y contando todos los objetos. A esto se le llama *contar todo*. Ahora su niño está aprendiendo una estrategia más rápida que le permite trabajar directamente con los números. El método que está aprendiendo se llama *contar hacia adelante*. Se explica a continuación.

En un problema de suma, como 5 + 4, los niños dicen (o "piensan") el primer número como si ya lo hubieran contado. Luego cuentan hacia adelante a partir de él. El último número que dicen es el total. Los niños pueden llevar la cuenta levantando un dedo o haciendo un punto por cada número mientras cuentan hacia adelante. El diagrama a continuación muestra tanto el método de los dedos como el de los puntos.

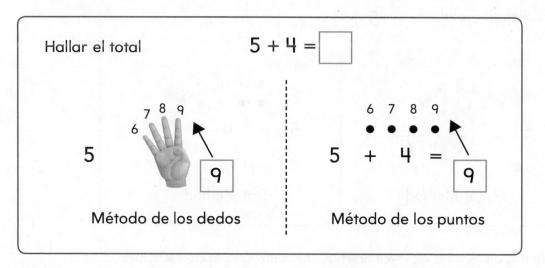

Contar hacia adelante requiere práctica. Esto sucede en las actividades de clase y tareas. En esta unidad, su niño está aprendiendo a hallar un total desconocido. En la próxima unidad, aprenderá a usar la estrategia de contar hacia adelante para restar.

Contar hacia adelante es un método que sirve como ayuda para que los niños dominen la suma y la resta en operaciones hasta el 10. La meta es lograr que al final del año escolar sepan automáticamente la respuesta cuando el total sea 10 ó menos.

Atentamente,
El maestro de su niño

© Houghton Mifflin Harcourt Publishing Company

Name _____

Count on. Write the total.

1 5 + 2 = ☐

5   ••

2 6 + 4 = ☐

6   ••••

3 8 + 1 = ☐

8   •

4 3 + 5 = ☐

3   •••••

5 7 + 3 = ☐

7   •••

6 2 + 2 = ☐

2   ••

7 4 + 5 = ☐

4   •••••

8 9 + 1 = ☐

9   •

9 3 + 2 = ☐

3   ••

10 5 + 1 = ☐

5   •

CC SS Content Standards **1.OA.C.5, 1.OA.C.6, 1.OA.D.8**
Mathematical Practices **MP6**

11 Solve.

$7 + 2 = \boxed{}$

Draw or write to explain how to count on.

Draw or write a different way to solve.

12 Choose a number 1, 2, 3, 4, or 5. Count on 3 more.
Complete the equation. Draw or write to explain.

$\boxed{} + 3 = \boxed{}$

 Check Understanding

Explain if you would use counting all or

counting on to solve $5 + 3 = \boxed{}$.

© Houghton Mifflin Harcourt Publishing Company

Explore Solution Methods

Name _____

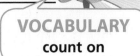

VOCABULARY
count on

Count on to find the total.

① 4 + 3 = ☐　　**②** 6 + 4 = ☐　　**③** 6 + 2 = ☐

④ 4 + 5 = ☐　　**⑤** 5 + 3 = ☐　　**⑥** 8 + 2 = ☐

⑦ 2 + 3 = ☐　　**⑧** 7 + 3 = ☐　　**⑨** 4 + 2 = ☐

Find the total number of toys.

⑩ 3 cars in the box

☐ Total

⑪ 7 boats in the box

☐ Total

⑫ 6 dolls in the box

☐ Total

⑬ 5 balls in the box

☐ Total

⑭ Write an equation that shows a total of 10. _____

Count on to find the total.

15 6 + 3 = ☐   16 5 + 2 = ☐   17 7 + 2 = ☐

18 7 + 3 = ☐   19 4 + 3 = ☐   20 4 + 5 = ☐

21 8 + 2 = ☐   22 5 + 2 = ☐   23 4 + 2 = ☐

24 5 + 3 = ☐   25 7 + 2 = ☐   26 7 + 3 = ☐

27 6 + 2 = ☐   28 6 + 4 = ☐   29 3 + 4 = ☐

PATH to FLUENCY **Add.**

1 7 + 0 = ☐   2 1 + 8 = ☐   3 0 + 8 = ☐

4 9 + 0 = ☐   5 7 + 1 = ☐   6 10 + 0 = ☐

7 6 + 1 = ☐   8 8 + 0 = ☐   9 8 + 1 = ☐

✔ **Check Understanding**
Draw dots to show how to count on
to solve 6 + 4 = ☐.

© Houghton Mifflin Harcourt Publishing Company

Addition Strategies: Counting On

Name _____

Underline the greater number.
Count on from that number.

1 3 + 7 = ☐

2 4 + 5 = ☐

3 2 + 6 = ☐

4 5 + 3 = ☐

5 7 + 2 = ☐

6 3 + 6 = ☐

7 5 + 2 = ☐

8 2 + 8 = ☐

9 7 + 3 = ☐

10 6 + 3 = ☐

11 Show two ways to count on to find the total of 6 + 3. Which is faster?

Underline the greater number.
Count on from that number.

12 <u>5</u> + 2 = ☐

13 7 + 3 = ☐

14 6 + 2 = ☐

15 5 + 3 = ☐

16 3 + 4 = ☐

17 2 + 7 = ☐

18 6 + 3 = ☐

19 8 + 2 = ☐

20 4 + 3 = ☐

21 2 + 5 = ☐

22 How did you solve Exercise 17?

 Check Understanding

To use counting on to solve $4 + 5 = $ ☐,
which number would you start with? Why?

Count On from the Greater Number

3 + 3 = ☐　　3 + 4 = ☐　　3 + 5 = ☐

3 + 6 = ☐　　3 + 7 = ☐　　4 + 3 = ☐

4 + 4 = ☐　　4 + 5 = ☐　　4 + 6 = ☐

5 + 3 = ☐　　5 + 4 = ☐　　5 + 5 = ☐

6 + 3 = ☐　　6 + 4 = ☐　　7 + 3 = ☐

$3 + 5 = \boxed{8}$

$\boxed{\text{•••}\,|\,5}$

$3 + 4 = \boxed{7}$

$\boxed{\text{•••}\,|\,4}$

$3 + 3 = \boxed{6}$

$\boxed{3\,|\,\text{•••}}$

$4 + 3 = \boxed{7}$

$\boxed{4\,|\,\text{•••}}$

$3 + 7 = \boxed{10}$

$\boxed{\text{•••}\,|\,7}$

$3 + 6 = \boxed{9}$

$\boxed{\text{•••}\,|\,6}$

$4 + 6 = \boxed{10}$

$\boxed{\text{••••}\,|\,6}$

$4 + 5 = \boxed{9}$

$\boxed{\text{••••}\,|\,5}$

$4 + 4 = \boxed{8}$

$\boxed{4\,|\,\text{••••}}$

$5 + 5 = \boxed{10}$

$\boxed{5\,|\,\text{•••••}}$

$5 + 4 = \boxed{9}$

$\boxed{5\,|\,\text{••••}}$

$5 + 3 = \boxed{8}$

$\boxed{5\,|\,\text{•••}}$

$7 + 3 = \boxed{10}$

$\boxed{7\,|\,\text{•••}}$

$6 + 4 = \boxed{10}$

$\boxed{6\,|\,\text{••••}}$

$6 + 3 = \boxed{9}$

$\boxed{6\,|\,\text{•••}}$

Red Count-On Cards

Number Quilt 1: Unknown Totals

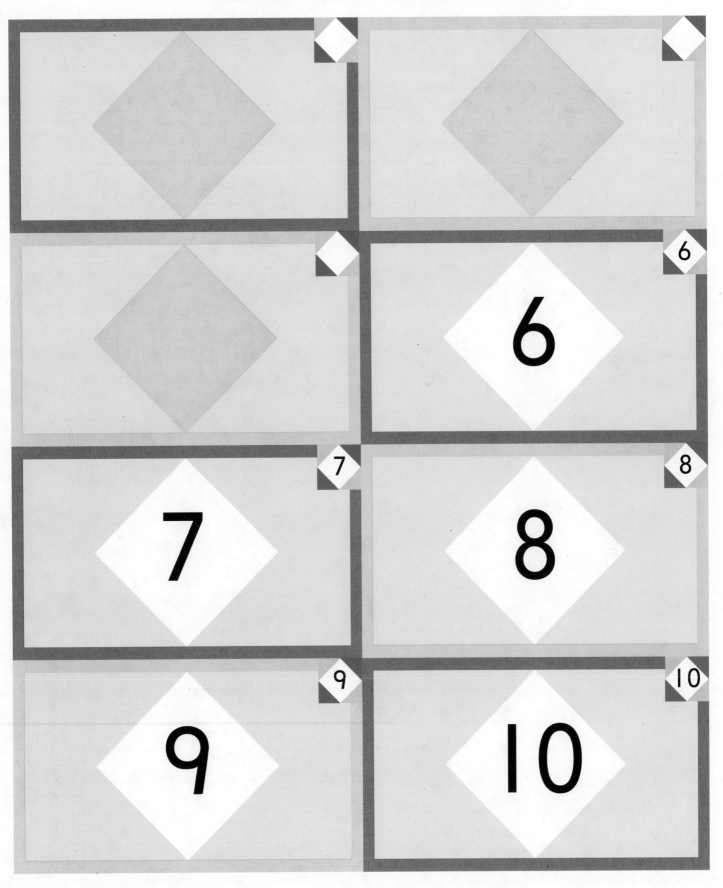

Use with Red Count-On Cards.

Number Quilt 1

Name _____

Draw more to count on. Write how many in all.

1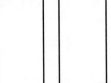

$4 + 1 = \boxed{}$

2

$6 + 2 = \boxed{}$

3

$3 + 3 = \boxed{}$

4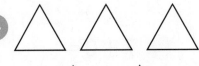

$5 + 4 = \boxed{}$

5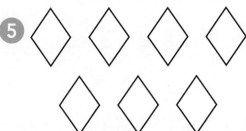

$7 + 3 = \boxed{}$

CC SS Content Standards **1.0A.B.3, 1.0A.C.5, 1.0A.C.6, 1.0A.D.8**
Mathematical Practices **MP1, MP8**

Underline the greater number.
Count on from that number.

6 $2 + \underline{8} = \boxed{}$ **7** $5 + 4 = \boxed{}$ **8** $6 + 3 = \boxed{}$

9 $7 + 3 = \boxed{}$ **10** $2 + 5 = \boxed{}$ **11** $3 + 4 = \boxed{}$

12 $4 + 3 = \boxed{}$ **13** $2 + 7 = \boxed{}$ **14** $8 + 2 = \boxed{}$

15 $3 + 6 = \boxed{}$ **16** $5 + 2 = \boxed{}$ **17** $6 + 2 = \boxed{}$

18 $5 + 3 = \boxed{}$ **19** $4 + 5 = \boxed{}$ **20** $2 + 6 = \boxed{}$

(PATH to FLUENCY) **Add.**

1 $3 + 2 = \boxed{}$ **2** $1 + 9 = \boxed{}$ **3** $7 + 0 = \boxed{}$

4 $8 + 1 = \boxed{}$ **5** $0 + 9 = \boxed{}$ **6** $1 + 6 = \boxed{}$

7 $8 + 0 = \boxed{}$ **8** $7 + 1 = \boxed{}$ **9** $2 + 3 = \boxed{}$

✓ **Check Understanding**

Explain how to count on to solve $6 + 3 = \boxed{}$ and
$2 + 8 = \boxed{}$.

      Addition Game: Unknown Totals

Name _____

Write the addition equation the model shows.

1

_____

Equation

2

_____

Equation

3

_____

Equation

4

_____

Equation

5

_____

Equation

CC SS Content Standards **1.OA.B.3, 1.OA.C.5, 1.OA.C.6, 1.OA.D.8**
Mathematical Practices **MP1, MP3, MP6**

Underline the greater addend in the equation.
Count on from that number and write the total.

6 6 + 3 = ☐

6 | ● ● ●

7 2 + 5 = ☐

● ● | 5

8 7 + 3 = ☐

7 | ● ● ●

9 5 + 3 = ☐

5 | ● ● ●

10 2 + 4 = ☐

● ● | 4

11 4 + 5 = ☐

● ● ● ● | 5

12 3 + 7 = ☐

● ● ● | 7

13 6 + 2 = ☐

6 | ● ●

14 4 + 6 = ☐

● ● ● ● | 6

15 7 + 2 = ☐

7 | ● ●

✓ **Check Understanding**

Draw circles to show counting on to solve
4 + 3 = ☐ and 2 + 7 = ☐.

Practice Counting On

Name _____   Date _____

Count on to find the total.

1 3 + 2 = ☐

2 6 + 1 = ☐

Underline the greater number.
Count on from that number.

3 4 + 5 = ☐

4 6 + 3 = ☐

Draw more to count on.
Write how many in all.

5 ○○○○○

5 + 2 = ☐

Name _____ Date _____

Add.

1 $5 + 0 = \boxed{}$

2 $0 + 6 = \boxed{}$

3 $0 + 8 = \boxed{}$

4 $9 + 0 = \boxed{}$

5 $0 + 10 = \boxed{}$

6 $9 + 1 = \boxed{}$

7 $1 + 3 = \boxed{}$

8 $2 + 1 = \boxed{}$

9 $2 + 3 = \boxed{}$

10 $1 + 5 = \boxed{}$

11 $4 + 0 = \boxed{}$

12 $7 + 1 = \boxed{}$

13 $3 + 2 = \boxed{}$

14 $1 + 9 = \boxed{}$

15 $8 + 1 = \boxed{}$

Name _____

Solve. Write how many are left.

1   There are 8 apples.

$8 - 5 = \boxed{}$

Then 5 are eaten.

2   There are 9 flowers.

$9 - 4 = \boxed{}$

Then 4 are picked.

3   There are 6 dolphins.

$6 - 3 = \boxed{}$

Then 3 swim away.

4   There are 10 balloons.

$10 - 6 = \boxed{}$

Then 6 pop.

5 You have 7 balls. You lose 2 balls. How many balls are left? Solve. Show your work.

Solve. Write how many are left.

6   There are 10 balloons.

$10 - 4 = \boxed{}$

Then 4 pop.

7   There are 8 apples.

$8 - 6 = \boxed{}$

Then 6 are eaten.

8 Look at Puzzled Penguin's work.

There were 7 flowers.

Then 3 were picked.

$7 - 3 = \boxed{3}$

Am I correct?

Help Puzzled Penguin.

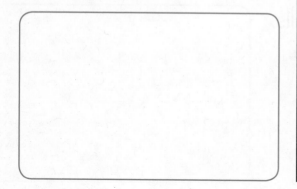

✔ **Check Understanding**
Draw circles to solve
$8 - 2 = \boxed{}$.

Represent Subtraction

Name _____

VOCABULARY
subtract

Subtract and write the equation.

1 Subtract 5

○○○○○ ○○○○

_____ Equation

2 Subtract 4

○○○○○ ○○○○○

_____ Equation

3 Subtract 3

○○○○○ ○○

_____ Equation

4 Subtract 8

○○○○○ ○○○○○

_____ Equation

5 Subtract 5

○○○○○ ○○○

_____ Equation

6 Subtract 7

○○○○○ ○○○○○

_____ Equation

7 Subtract 6

○○○○○ ○○○○

_____ Equation

Subtract and write the equation.

8   Subtract 5

○○○○○ ○○○

Equation _____

9   Subtract 3

○○○○○ · ○○○○

Equation _____

10   Subtract 6

○○○○○ ○○○○○

Equation _____

11   Subtract 4

○○○○○ ○○

Equation _____

12   Subtract 2

○○○○○ ○○○○

Equation _____

13 There are 6 toy trucks on the table. 4 trucks roll off. How many toy trucks are there now? Use a circle drawing to solve. Then write the equation.

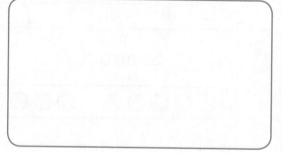

 Check Understanding

Make a circle drawing to show 10 − 7 = 3.

Subtraction with Drawings and Equations

Name _____

Use the picture to solve the equation.

 ⬤⬤⬤⬤⬤　⬤⬤⬤⬤

$$9 - 6 = \boxed{}$$

 ⬤⬤⬤⬤⬤　⬤⬤⬤

$$8 - 5 = \boxed{}$$

 ⬤⬤⬤⬤

$$4 - 4 = \boxed{}$$

 ⬤⬤⬤⬤⬤　⬤⬤

$$7 - 3 = \boxed{}$$

 ⬤⬤⬤⬤⬤　⬤

$$6 - 5 = \boxed{}$$

 ⬤⬤⬤⬤⬤

$$5 - 4 = \boxed{}$$

 ⬤⬤⬤⬤⬤　⬤⬤⬤⬤⬤

$$10 - 6 = \boxed{}$$

 ⬤⬤⬤⬤⬤　⬤⬤⬤⬤

$$9 - 3 = \boxed{}$$

 ⬤⬤⬤⬤⬤　⬤⬤

$$7 - 6 = \boxed{}$$

 ⬤⬤⬤⬤⬤　⬤⬤⬤⬤⬤

$$10 - 2 = \boxed{}$$

 ⬤⬤⬤⬤⬤　⬤⬤⬤

$$8 - 4 = \boxed{}$$

 ⬤⬤⬤⬤⬤　⬤

$$6 - 2 = \boxed{}$$

Use the picture to solve the equation.

13

$$5 - 3 = \boxed{}$$

14

$$7 - 4 = \boxed{}$$

15

$$9 - 5 = \boxed{}$$

16

$$6 - 4 = \boxed{}$$

17

$$10 - 3 = \boxed{}$$

18

$$8 - 6 = \boxed{}$$

19 Make a circle drawing for the equation $6 - 2 = \boxed{}$. Then find the answer.

PATH to FLUENCY Subtract.

1 $2 - 1 = \boxed{}$ **2** $6 - 0 = \boxed{}$ **3** $1 - 0 = \boxed{}$

4 $4 - 1 = \boxed{}$ **5** $3 - 1 = \boxed{}$ **6** $10 - 0 = \boxed{}$

 Check Understanding

Listen to the story. Write and solve the equation for the story.

Practice with Subtraction

Name _____

Write the equation for the story problem. Draw circles to prove if the equation is true or false.

1 There are 8 people at the party.
Then 2 people leave. Now there are
6 people at the party.

_____
Equation

2 There are 6 cups on the table.
Tim puts 3 cups in the dishwasher.
Now there are 2 cups on the table.

_____
Equation

3 There are 7 birds in the tree. 4 fly away.
Now there are 4 birds in the tree.

_____
Equation

Circle if the equation is true or false.
Draw to explain.

4 $9 - 4 = 7 - 1$

true   false

5 $6 - 3 = 8 - 5$

true   false

6 $4 - 1 = 5 - 2$

true   false

7 $7 - 2 = 9 - 4$

true   false

8 $3 - 1 = 4 - 1$

true   false

9 $6 - 3 = 8 - 6$

true   false

 Check Understanding

Make a circle drawing to show $9 - 6 = \boxed{}$.

Generate Subtraction Problems

Write how many are left.

Use the picture to help you.

1 There are 7 fish.

Then 3 swim away.

$7 - 3 = \boxed{}$

---

2 There are 10 snails.

Then 5 crawl away.

$10 - 5 = \boxed{}$

Use the picture to solve the equation.

 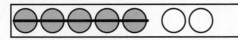

$7 - 5 = \boxed{}$

Subtract and write the equation.

Subtract 4   _____

                              Equation

 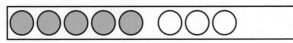

Subtract 6   _____

                              Equation

Name _____ Date _____

Subtract.

1 1 − 0 = ☐   **2** 3 − 1 = ☐   **3** 2 − 0 = ☐

4 4 − 1 = ☐   **5** 6 − 0 = ☐   **6** 5 − 1 = ☐

7 7 − 0 = ☐   **8** 8 − 1 = ☐   **9** 9 − 1 = ☐

10 8 − 0 = ☐   **11** 9 − 0 = ☐   **12** 7 − 1 = ☐

13 10 − 0 = ☐   **14** 6 − 1 = ☐   **15** 10 − 1 = ☐

Name _____

Relate addition and subtraction.

1

Addition	Subtraction

Addition

5 cats are here.

3 cats come.

How many cats in all?

$5 + 3 =$ ●●●●● | ○○○

$5 + 3 = \square$

$5 + 3 = \boxed{}$

Total Unknown

Subtraction

8 cats are here.

5 cats run away.

How many cats are left?

$8 - 5 =$ ●●●●● ○○○

$8 - 5 = \square$

$8 - 5 = \boxed{}$

Partner Unknown

$5 + \square = 8$

Use addition to solve subtraction.

2 $4 + 4 = 8$, so I know $8 - 4 = \boxed{}$.

3 $6 + 3 = 9$, so I know $9 - 6 = \boxed{}$.

4 $7 + 3 = 10$, so I know $10 - 7 = \boxed{}$.

5 $5 + 4 = 9$, so I know $9 - 5 = \boxed{}$.

6 $3 + 3 = 6$, so I know $6 - 3 = \boxed{}$.

Equations	Vertical Forms
5 + 3 = 8	5 8
8 − 5 = 3	+ 3 − 5
	8 3

Solve the vertical form. Use any method.

7. 6
   + 4

8. 7
   + 2

9. 1
   + 6

10. 2
    + 6

11. 3
    + 7

Solve the vertical form. Think about addition.

12. 10
    − 8

13. 9
    − 5

14. 7
    − 1

15. 8
    − 3

16. 10
    − 5

PATH to FLUENCY Subtract.

1. 4 − 0 = ☐

2. 6 − 1 = ☐

3. 4 − 2 = ☐

4. 9 − 1 = ☐

5. 5 − 2 = ☐

6. 8 − 0 = ☐

7. 3 − 2 = ☐

8. 9 − 0 = ☐

9. 7 − 1 = ☐

 Check Understanding

Write the related subtraction equation for
5 + 4 = 9. Write the vertical form.

Relate Addition and Subtraction

Name _____

Write and solve equations and vertical forms.

1 There are 3 pink flowers and 4 yellow flowers in the garden. How many flowers are there in all?

_____
Equation

2 Olivia made 4 clay animals. She made 1 green clay animal. How many clay animals are not green?

_____
Equation

3 There are 6 turtles in the water and 2 turtles crawl out of the water. How many turtles are in the water now?

_____
Equation

Solve.

4 Use the picture to write a story problem.

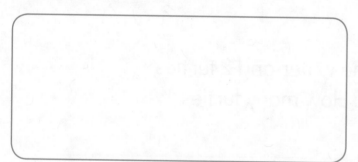

_____

- -

_____

- -

_____

- -

_____

5 Write and solve equations and vertical forms
for the problem created.

_____

Equation

✓ **Check Understanding**

Solve $7 - 3 = \square$. Write the vertical form.

Mixed Practice with Equations

Name _____

Darya and her family go to the animal park.

Use the picture to solve the equation.

1 Darya sees 5 lions. Then she sees 3 more lions.

How many lions does she see in all?   5 + 3 = ☐

---

2 Nick sees 9 crocodiles in the water.

Then 2 crocodiles climb out.

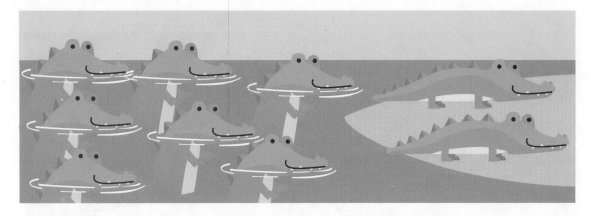

How many crocodiles are in the water now?   9 − 2 = ☐

CC SS Content Standards **1.OA.A.1, 1.OA.C.6, 1.OA.D.8**
Mathematical Practices **MP1, MP4, MP5**

Use the picture to solve the equation.

3 Ray sees 1 cheetah in a tree and 7 lions under a tree.

How many wild cats does he see?   1 + 7 = ☐

---

4 Sophie sees 8 baboons and 2 mandrills.

How many monkeys does she see?   8 + 2 = ☐

Focus on Mathematical Practices

Name _____   Date _____

Use addition to solve subtraction.

1 $5 + 3 = 8$, so I know $8 - 3 = $ ☐ .

2 $6 + 4 = 10$, so I know $10 - 4 = $ ☐ .

Solve the vertical form.
Think about addition.

3
$$\begin{array}{r} 6 \\ -\,2 \\ \hline \end{array}$$

4
$$\begin{array}{r} 8 \\ -\,1 \\ \hline \end{array}$$

5
$$\begin{array}{r} 9 \\ -\,7 \\ \hline \end{array}$$

Name _____

Date _____

PATH to FLUENCY

Subtract.

1 1 − 1 = ☐   **2** 2 − 0 = ☐   **3** 2 − 1 = ☐

4 4 − 1 = ☐   **5** 3 − 1 = ☐   **6** 5 − 0 = ☐

7 3 − 2 = ☐   **8** 5 − 1 = ☐   **9** 6 − 0 = ☐

10 7 − 0 = ☐   **11** 4 − 2 = ☐   **12** 6 − 1 = ☐

13 8 − 1 = ☐   **14** 9 − 0 = ☐   **15** 5 − 2 = ☐

Write the partners and the total.

1 ☐ + ☐

Total ☐

2 ☐ + ☐

Total ☐

3 Does the equation match the circle drawing?
Choose Yes or No.

$3 + 2 = 5$

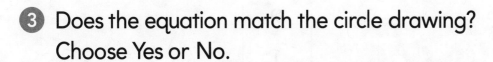

○ Yes ○ No

$5 + 2 = 7$

○ Yes ○ No

$6 + 3 = 9$

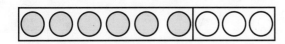

○ Yes ○ No

Ring the total number of toys in the group.

4 7 dolls in the box

7
9
0 Total

---

5 4 boats in the box

7
9
I Total

---

6 Ring a number to show the cars
in the box. Write the total.

4
5
6

☐ Total

7 Solve. Match the story or circle drawing to the equation.

There are 8 apples.

 •

• $9 - 3 = 6$

Then 3 are eaten.

There are 7 flowers.

 •

• $10 - 6 = 4$

Then 5 are picked.

Subtract 3

   •

• $7 - 5 = 2$

Subtract 6

   •

• $8 - 3 = 5$

8 Make a circle drawing.

for the equation $6 - 4 = \boxed{}$.

Then find the answer.

9 Write the subtraction equation below the addition equation that helps you solve it.

$10 - 2 = 8$	$8 - 5 = 3$	$9 - 4 = 5$

$3 + 5 = 8$ $\qquad$ $5 + 4 = 9$ $\qquad$ $8 + 2 = 10$

_____ $\qquad$ _____ $\qquad$ _____

10 Write an equation for the story. Make a
Proof Drawing to show that the equation is true.
Write the vertical form.

> There are 7 flowers in the vase.
>
> Lily puts 2 more flowers in the vase.
>
> Now there are 9 flowers.

How Many?

1 Take some red cubes.
Write the number of red cubes. _____

2 Take some blue cubes.
Write the number of blue cubes. _____

3 Draw to show the red cubes and blue cubes.

4 Write an equation that shows how many cubes in all.

_____ + _____ = _____

5 Tell how you added the cubes.

_____

_____

6 Write a subtraction equation.
Make a Proof Drawing to solve it.

_____ − _____ = _____

7 Tell how you subtracted the circles.

_____

_____

8 **Part A**

Write an addition story.

_____

_____

Part B

Write an equation to show your addition story.
Make a Proof Drawing of your addition story.

_____ + _____ = _____

Tell how you solved your addition story.

9 **Part A**

Look at the numbers you used in your addition story.
Use the same numbers to write a subtraction story.

_____

_____

_____

Part B

Write an equation to show your subtraction story.
Make a Proof Drawing of your subtraction story.

_____ – _____ = _____

Tell how you solved your subtraction story.

Dear Family:

Your child has started a new unit on story problems. Because most children this age are learning to read, your child may need help reading the story problems. Offer help when it is needed, but do not give the answer.

To solve story problems, children first need to know which number is unknown. Is it the total or one of the parts? This program helps children focus on this important issue by using "Math Mountains." In a Math Mountain, the total sits at the top and the parts (or partners) sit at the bottom of the mountain. Children can quickly see the relationship between the partners and the total when they look at the mountain.

Math Mountain

Math Mountains are especially helpful in showing children how to find an unknown partner, as in the following problem: *I see 9 horses. 5 are black, and the others are white. How many horses are white?*

Children can find the answer by drawing the mountain to see which number is unknown. Then they count on from the partner they know to the total. In this way, they can find the partner they don't know.

Math Mountain with
Unknown Partner

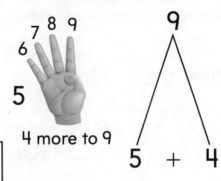

If you have any questions, please contact me.

Sincerely,
Your child's teacher

© Houghton Mifflin Harcourt Publishing Company

CCSS Unit 3 addresses the following standards from the Common Core State Standards for Mathematics: **1.OA.A.1, 1.OA.B.3, 1.OA.B.4, 1.OA.C.5, 1.OA.C.6, 1.OA.D.7, 1.OA.D.8, and all** Mathematical Practices.

Estimada familia:

Su niño ha empezado una nueva unidad donde aprenderá cómo resolver problemas matemáticos. Como la mayoría de los niños a esta edad aún están aprendiendo a leer, es probable que su niño necesite ayuda para leer los problemas. Ofrezca ayuda cuando haga falta, pero no dé la respuesta.

Para resolver problemas, los niños primero deben hallar el número desconocido. ¿Es el total o una de las partes? Este programa los ayuda a concentrarse en este punto importante usando "Montañas matemáticas". En una montaña matemática el total está en la cima y las partes están al pie de la montaña. Al ver la montaña, los niños pueden ver rápidamente la relación entre las partes y el total.

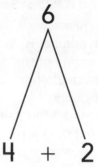

Montaña
matemática

Las montañas matemáticas son especialmente útiles para mostrar a los niños cómo hallar una parte desconocida, como en el problema siguiente: *Veo 9 caballos. 5 son negros y los demás son blancos. ¿Cuántos caballos son blancos?*

Los niños pueden hallar la respuesta dibujando la montaña para saber cuál es el número desconocido. Luego, cuentan hacia adelante a partir de la parte que conocen para hallar el total. De esta manera, pueden hallar la parte desconocida.

Montaña matemática
con parte
desconocida

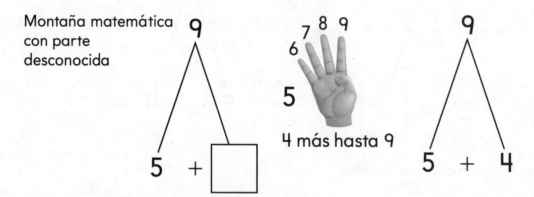

Si tiene alguna pregunta, por favor comuníquese conmigo.

Atentamente,
El maestro de su niño

CC SS En la Unidad 3 se aplican los siguientes estándares de los Estándares estatales comunes de matemáticas **1.OA.A.1, 1.OA.B.3, 1.OA.B.4, 1.OA.C.5, 1.OA.C.6, 1.OA.D.7, 1.OA.D.8** y todos los de Prácticas matemáticas.

subtraction
story problem

8 flies are on a log.
6 are eaten by a frog.
How many flies are left?

Name _____

Find the unknown partner.

1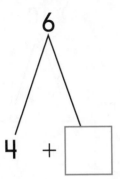
6
4 + ☐

2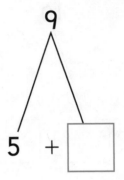
9
5 + ☐

3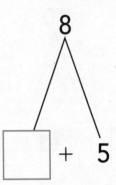
8
☐ + 5

4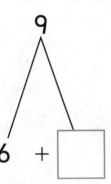
9
6 + ☐

5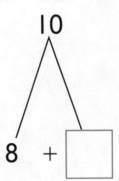
10
8 + ☐

6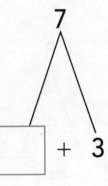
7
☐ + 3

7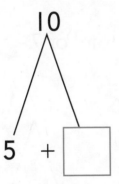
10
5 + ☐

8
8
☐ + 6

9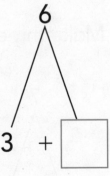
6
3 + ☐

10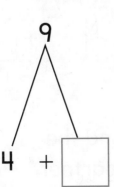
9
4 + ☐

11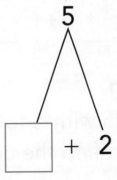
5
☐ + 2

12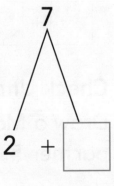
7
2 + ☐

13 Make three different Math Mountains with a total of 10.

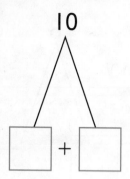 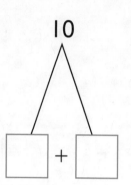 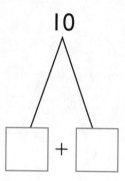

14 Make three different Math Mountains with a total of 8.

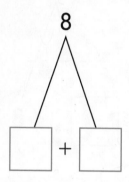 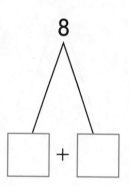 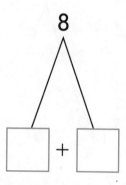

15 Make three different Math Mountains with a total of 7.

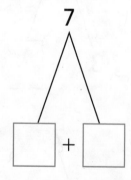 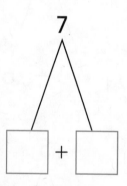 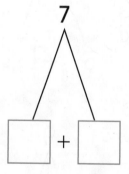

✓ **Check Understanding**

Draw a Math Mountain with a total of 8 and the partner 5. Count on to find the unknown partner.

Explore Unknowns

Name _____

Solve the story problem.

Show your work. Use drawings, numbers, or words.

1. We see 9 fish.
   5 are big. The others are small.
   How many fish are small?

   fish

   [ ] _____
   label

2. 8 boys are riding bikes.
   6 ride fast. The rest ride slow.
   How many boys ride slow?

   bike

   [ ] _____
   label

3. Ana has 2 hats.
   Then she gets more.
   Now she has 5.
   How many hats does she get?

   hat

   [ ] _____
   label

4. Why is it important to write a
   label in the answer?

   _____

   _____

Solve the story problem. Use cubes to help.

5 Raja has 6 peaches. He wants to put some on each of two plates. How many can he put on each plate? Show 4 answers.

$6 = \boxed{} + \boxed{}$

$6 = \boxed{} + \boxed{}$

$6 = \boxed{} + \boxed{}$

$6 = \boxed{} + \boxed{}$

✔ **Check Understanding**

Kelly has 5 cubes. He gives some to Maria and some to Jake. How many cubes can he give to each person? Find 3 answers.

Problems with Unknown Partners

Name _____

Count on to find the unknown partner.

1 3 + ☐ = 6

2 7 + ☐ = 10

3 2 + ☐ = 6

4 7 + ☐ = 9

5 4 + ☐ = 8

6 5 + ☐ = 8

Count on to solve.

7 6 letters total

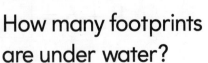 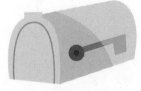

How many letters are in the box? ☐ _____
label

---

8 10 footprints total

How many footprints are under water? ☐ _____
label

CCSS Content Standards **1.0A.C.5, 1.0A.C.6, 1.0A.D.8**
Mathematical Practices **MP1, MP2, MP3, MP6**

9 Look at Puzzled Penguin's work.

$2 +$ ☐ $= 8$

$2 +$ $\boxed{10}$ $= 8$

Am I correct?

---

10 Help Puzzled Penguin.

$2 +$ ☐ $= 8$

PATH to FLUENCY Add.

1 $4 + 4 =$ ☐   **2** $3 + 7 =$ ☐   **3** $3 + 3 =$ ☐

4 $8 + 2 =$ ☐   **5** $2 + 2 =$ ☐   **6** $6 + 4 =$ ☐

7 $1 + 1 =$ ☐   **8** $1 + 9 =$ ☐   **9** $5 + 5 =$ ☐

10 $7 + 3 =$ ☐   **11** $2 + 8 =$ ☐   **12** $4 + 6 =$ ☐

✔ **Check Understanding**

Explain how to count on using dots to

solve the equation $6 +$ ☐ $= 10$.

Solve Equations with Unknown Partners

$3 + \boxed{} = 6$

$3 + \boxed{} = 7$

$3 + \boxed{} = 8$

$3 + \boxed{} = 9$

$3 + \boxed{} = 10$

$4 + \boxed{} = 7$

$4 + \boxed{} = 8$

$4 + \boxed{} = 9$

$4 + \boxed{} = 10$

$5 + \boxed{} = 8$

$5 + \boxed{} = 9$

$5 + \boxed{} = 10$

$6 + \boxed{} = 9$

$6 + \boxed{} = 10$

$7 + \boxed{} = 10$

$3 + \boxed{5} = 8$

$\boxed{3}$ •••••

$3 + \boxed{4} = 7$

$\boxed{3}$ ••••

$3 + \boxed{3} = 6$

$\boxed{3}$ •••

$4 + \boxed{3} = 7$

$\boxed{4}$ •••

$3 + \boxed{7} = 10$

$\boxed{3}$ •••••••

$3 + \boxed{6} = 9$

$\boxed{3}$ ••••••

$4 + \boxed{6} = 10$

$\boxed{4}$ ••••••

$4 + \boxed{5} = 9$

$\boxed{4}$ •••••

$4 + \boxed{4} = 8$

$\boxed{4}$ ••••

$5 + \boxed{5} = 10$

$\boxed{5}$ •••••

$5 + \boxed{4} = 9$

$\boxed{5}$ ••••

$5 + \boxed{3} = 8$

$\boxed{5}$ •••

$7 + \boxed{3} = 10$

$\boxed{7}$ •••

$6 + \boxed{4} = 10$

$\boxed{6}$ ••••

$6 + \boxed{3} = 9$

$\boxed{6}$ •••

Yellow Count-On Cards

Number Quilt 2: Unknown Partners

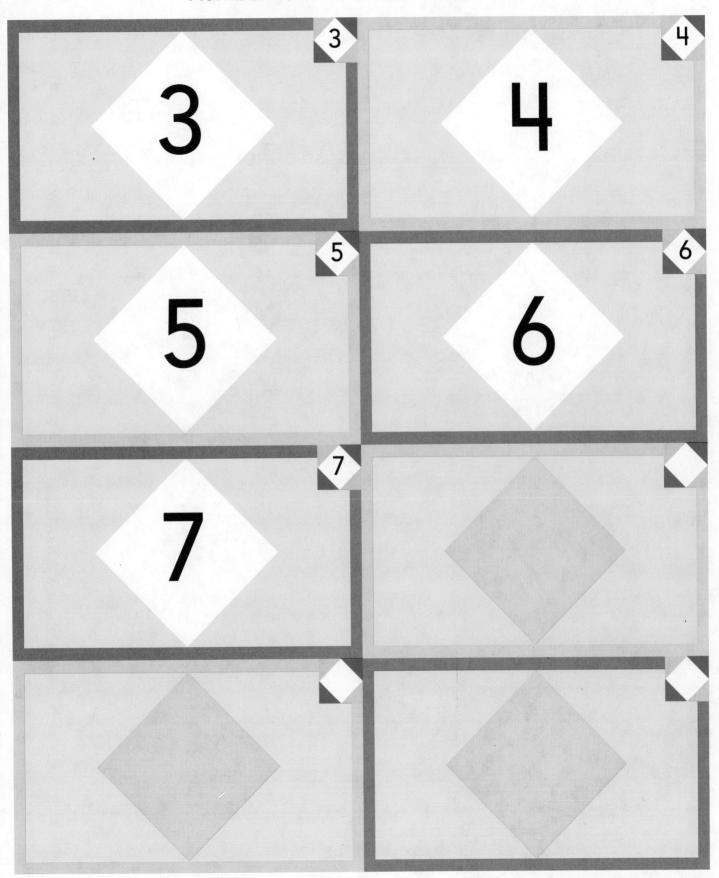

Use with the Yellow or Orange Count-On Cards.

Name _____

Solve the story problem.

Show your work. Use drawings, numbers, or words.

1 Sam has 4 balloons.
Then he gets some more.
Now he has 9.
How many balloons does he get?

balloon

☐ _____
        label

2 There are 8 crayons on the table.
There are 5 red crayons.
The others are green.
How many crayons are green?

table

☐ _____
        label

3 Rabia sees 10 eagles.
There are 3 in a tree.
The rest are flying.
How many eagles are flying?

eagle

☐ _____
        label

Solve the story problem.

Show your work. Use drawings, numbers, or words.

4 Maddox has 3 toy trains.
Then he gets more.
Now he has 7.
How many trains does he get?

train

☐ _____
　　　　　label

5 We pick 10 apples from the trees.
6 are green. Some are red.
How many apples are red?

tree

☐ _____
　　　　　label

6 Milena wants to put 8 balls
in a box. She wants to have
soccer balls and footballs.
How many of each ball could
she use? Show two answers.

soccer ball

☐ soccer balls and ☐ footballs

or ☐ soccer balls and ☐ footballs

✔ **Check Understanding**
Write the unknown partner.　$4 + \boxed{} = 10$

　　　Addition Game: Unknown Partners

Name _____

Draw a Math Mountain, and write an equation to represent the story.

1. There are 8 cows in the field. There are 6 brown cows. The rest are black. How many cows are black?

_____
Equation

2. There are 5 kittens sleeping. Some more join them. Now there are 9 kittens sleeping. How many kittens join?

_____
Equation

3. Jenny has 7 flowers. She wants to put some flowers in a red vase and a pink vase. How many flowers can she put in each vase?

_____
Equation

CC SS Content Standards **1.OA.A.1, 1.OA.C.6, 1.OA.D.8**
Mathematical Practices **MP2, MP6**

Draw a Math Mountain for the equation.

4 $6 + \square = 10$

5 $7 + \square = 10$

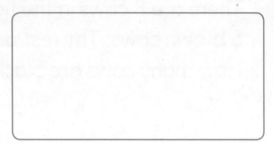

6 $5 + \square = 10$

7 $9 + \square = 10$

8 $4 + \square = 10$

9 $2 + \square = 10$

✓ Check Understanding

Draw a Math Mountain that matches the equation $7 + \square = 9$.

Practice with Unknown Partners

Name _____ Date _____

Count on to find the unknown partner.

1 $2 + \boxed{} = 5$ | **2** $4 + \boxed{} = 7$ | **3** $5 + \boxed{} = 9$

Count on to solve.

4 7 pencils total

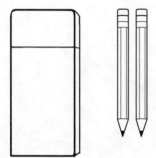

How many pencils are in the box?

$\boxed{}$ _____
label

5 10 pennies total

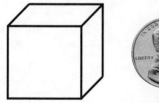

How many pennies are in the box?

$\boxed{}$ _____
label

Name _____ Date _____

Add.

1 $1 + 1 = $ ☐   **2** $2 + 8 = $ ☐   **3** $8 + 2 = $ ☐

4 $3 + 7 = $ ☐   **5** $2 + 2 = $ ☐   **6** $1 + 9 = $ ☐

7 $0 + 10 = $ ☐   **8** $4 + 6 = $ ☐   **9** $3 + 3 = $ ☐

10 $9 + 1 = $ ☐   **11** $4 + 4 = $ ☐   **12** $6 + 4 = $ ☐

13 $5 + 5 = $ ☐   **14** $10 + 0 = $ ☐   **15** $7 + 3 = $ ☐

VOCABULARY
subtraction story problem

Solve the **subtraction story problem**.   Show your work. Use drawings, numbers, or words.

1 8 flies are on a log.
A frog eats 6 of them.
How many flies are left?

frog

☐ _____
label

---

2 I find 7 shells by the sea.
Then I lose 3 of them.
How many shells do I
have now?

shell

☐ _____
label

---

3 I draw 10 houses.
Then I erase 5 of them.
How many houses are left?

house

☐ _____
label

Content Standards **1.OA.A.1, 1.OA.B.4, 1.OA.C.6, 1.OA.D.8**
Mathematical Practices **MP1, MP4**

4 Write a subtraction story problem.

_____

- -

_____

_____

- -

_____

_____

- -

_____

5 Write an equation to solve the story problem.
Use a box for the unknown number.

PATH to FLUENCY Subtract.

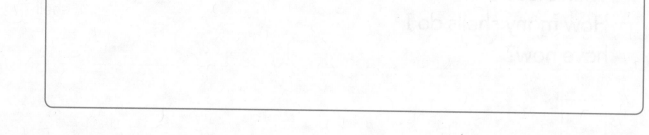

1 6 – 5 = ☐   **2** 2 – 1 = ☐   **3** 8 – 7 = ☐

4 10 – 9 = ☐   **5** 5 – 4 = ☐   **6** 3 – 2 = ☐

✓ **Check Understanding**

Listen to the subtraction story. Write an equation
to solve. Use a box for the unknown number.

Subtraction Strategies

$6 - 3 = \square$

$7 - 3 = \square$

$8 - 3 = \square$

$9 - 3 = \square$

$10 - 3 = \square$

$7 - 4 = \square$

$8 - 4 = \square$

$9 - 4 = \square$

$10 - 4 = \square$

$8 - 5 = \square$

$9 - 5 = \square$

$10 - 5 = \square$

$9 - 6 = \square$

$10 - 6 = \square$

$10 - 7 = \square$

$8 - 3 = \boxed{5}$

$\boxed{3}\,|\,\bullet\bullet\bullet\bullet\bullet$

$7 - 3 = \boxed{4}$

$\boxed{3}\,|\,\bullet\bullet\bullet\bullet$

$6 - 3 = \boxed{3}$

$\boxed{3}\,|\,\bullet\bullet\bullet$

$7 - 4 = \boxed{3}$

$\boxed{4}\,|\,\bullet\bullet\bullet$

$10 - 3 = \boxed{7}$

$\boxed{3}\,|\,\bullet\bullet\bullet\bullet\,\bullet\bullet\bullet$

$9 - 3 = \boxed{6}$

$\boxed{3}\,|\,\bullet\,\bullet\bullet\bullet\bullet\bullet$

$10 - 4 = \boxed{6}$

$\boxed{4}\,|\,\bullet\bullet\,\bullet\bullet\bullet\bullet$

$9 - 4 = \boxed{5}$

$\boxed{4}\,|\,\bullet\bullet\bullet\bullet\bullet$

$8 - 4 = \boxed{4}$

$\boxed{4}\,|\,\bullet\bullet\bullet\bullet$

$10 - 5 = \boxed{5}$

$\boxed{5}\,|\,\bullet\bullet\bullet\bullet\bullet$

$9 - 5 = \boxed{4}$

$\boxed{5}\,|\,\bullet\bullet\bullet\bullet$

$8 - 5 = \boxed{3}$

$\boxed{5}\,|\,\bullet\bullet\bullet$

$10 - 7 = \boxed{3}$

$\boxed{7}\,|\,\bullet\bullet\bullet$

$10 - 6 = \boxed{4}$

$\boxed{6}\,|\,\bullet\bullet\bullet\bullet$

$9 - 6 = \boxed{3}$

$\boxed{6}\,|\,\bullet\bullet\bullet$

Orange Count-On Cards

Name _____

Solve. Make a drawing, and write an equation.

1 There are 9 stickers on the sheet.
John uses 6 stickers. How many
stickers are left?

☐ _____   _____

          label   Equation

2 Cody sees 7 bees on flowers.
Then 3 bees fly away. How many
bees are there now?

☐ _____   _____

          label   Equation

3 The tomato plant has 5 tomatoes.
Marvin picks 2 tomatoes. How
many tomatoes are left?

☐ _____   _____

          label   Equation

CC SS Content Standards 1.OA.A.1, 1.OA.B.4, 1.OA.C.5, 1.OA.C.6, 1.OA.D.8
Mathematical Practices MP1, MP4, MP5

Count on to find the partner.

4 6 − 3 = ☐

| 3 | • • • |

5 7 − 5 = ☐

| 5 | • • |

6 7 − 3 = ☐

| 3 | • • • • |

7 5 − 3 = ☐

| 3 | • • |

8 9 − 5 = ☐

| 5 | • • • • |

9 8 − 4 = ☐

| 4 | • • • • |

10 10 − 7 = ☐

| 7 | • • • |

11 9 − 6 = ☐

| 6 | • • • |

✔ Check Understanding

Explain how to solve the subtraction

problem 9 − 4 = ☐.

Subtraction Stories and Games

Name _____

Solve and discuss.

1 We see 10 dogs.
Then 7 run away.
How many are left?

☐ _____
     label

_____
Equation

_____
Equation

_____

2 We see 9 dogs.
There are 5 not barking.
The rest are barking.
How many are barking?

☐ _____
     label

_____
Equation

_____
Equation

_____

3 Discuss the methods you used to solve the problems.
How are they alike and different?

CC SS Content Standards **1.0A.A.1, 1.0A.B.4, 1.0A.D.8**
Mathematical Practices **MP3, MP6, MP8**

Practice with Subtraction Stories **119**

Solve the story problem.

Show your work. Use drawings, numbers, or words.

4 There are 8 apples. 6 apples are eaten.
How many apples are there now?

apple

☐ _____
label

5 There are 10 birds in the tree.
6 are singing. The rest are not singing.
How many birds are not singing?

tree

☐ _____
label

6 Liam has 8 carrots. He eats 4 carrots.
How many carrots are left?

carrot

☐ _____
label

✓ **Check Understanding**
Solve the problem. Write the equation.
We see 9 bunnies in the grass.
3 are hopping. The rest are not hopping.
How many bunnies are not hopping?

bunny

☐ _____
label

_____
Equation

Practice with Subtraction Stories

Subtract.

1 $6 - 3 = \boxed{}$

2 $7 - 2 = \boxed{}$

3 $10 - 4 = \boxed{}$

Solve the story problem.

Show your work.

4 Corey has 9 grapes.
He eats 5 of them.
How many grapes are left?

$\boxed{}$ _____
label

---

5 There are 8 kittens.
6 kittens are black.
The rest are white.
How many kittens are white?

$\boxed{}$ _____
label

Name _____ Date _____

PATH to
FLUENCY

Subtract.

1 2 − 1 = ☐   **2** 4 − 3 = ☐   **3** 3 − 2 = ☐

4 7 − 6 = ☐   **5** 6 − 5 = ☐   **6** 5 − 4 = ☐

7 9 − 8 = ☐   **8** 8 − 7 = ☐   **9** 10 − 9 = ☐

10 4 − 3 = ☐   **11** 6 − 5 = ☐   **12** 2 − 1 = ☐

13 5 − 4 = ☐   **14** 10 − 9 = ☐   **15** 7 − 6 = ☐

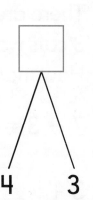

Solve and discuss.

1 There are 4 cats. Then
3 more cats join them.
How many cats are there now?

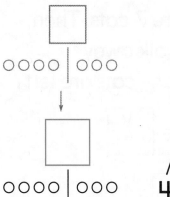

$4 + 3 = \boxed{}$

---

2 There are 6 cats.
Some more cats join them.
Now there are 8 cats.
How many cats join?

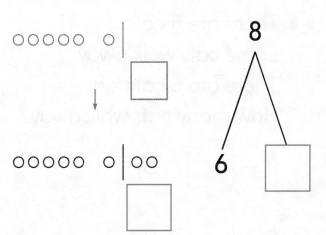

$6 + \boxed{} = 8$

---

3 There are some cats.
Then 4 more cats join them.
Now there are 9 cats.
How many cats are there
at the start?

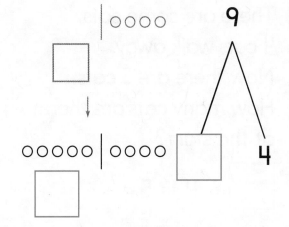

$\boxed{} + 4 = 9$

Solve and discuss.

4 There are 7 cats. Then
3 cats walk away.
How many cats are left?

$7 - 3 = \boxed{}$

$3 + \boxed{} = 7$

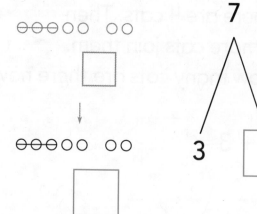

---

5 There are 8 cats.
Some cats walk away.
There are 6 cats left.
How many cats walk away?

$8 - \boxed{} = 6$

$6 + \boxed{} = 8$

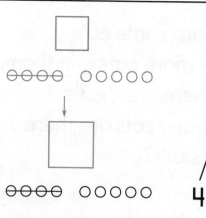

---

6 There are some cats.
4 cats walk away.
Now there are 5 cats.
How many cats are there
at the start?

$\boxed{} - 4 = 5$

$5 + 4 = \boxed{}$

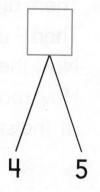

Relate Addition and Subtraction Situations

Name _____

Solve the story problem.

Show your work. Use drawings, numbers, or words.

7 There are 10 kittens. There are 7 playing.
The rest are sleeping.
How many are sleeping?

kitten

☐ _____
label

8 Emma has 5 beads. She gets some more
beads. Now she has 9 beads. How many
beads does she get?

bead

☐ _____
label

9 There are 8 boys at the park. Some boys go
home. Now 3 boys are left. How many boys
go home?

boy

☐ _____
label

10 Some horses are in the barn. Then 3 more
horses go in. Now 7 horses are in the barn.
How many are there at the start?

barn

☐ _____
label

Relate Addition and Subtraction Situations **125**

Solve the story problem.

11 Dad picks some flowers. He puts 2 in the red vase and the other 5 in the blue vase. How many does he pick?

flower

□ _____
label

12 Meg has some cherries. She eats 6. There are 4 left. How many did she have at first?

cherry

□ _____
label

13 There are 5 puppies. Then 3 more puppies come. How many puppies are there now?

puppy

□ _____
label

 Check Understanding

Listen to the story problem. Draw a picture and write both a subtraction and an addition equation to solve the story problem.

Relate Addition and Subtraction Situations

Solve.

1 Sam scores 4 points. Julio scores 3 points.
How many points do they score in all?

| Sam _____ | Julio _____ | Together ☐ |

2 Sam scores 4 points. Julio also scores some points. In all
they score 7 points. How many points does Julio score?

| Sam _____ | Julio ☐ | Together _____ |

3 Sam scores some points. Then Julio scores 3 points. In all
they score 7 points. How many points does Sam score?

| Sam ☐ | Julio _____ | Together _____ |

Solve the story problem.

Show your work. Use drawings, numbers, or words.

4 8 frogs are in the pond. Some hop away.
2 are left. How many frogs hop away?

pond

☐ _____
label

5 Ivan has some balls. He gives 4 to friends.
He has 3 left. How many did he have before?

ball

☐ _____
label

6 There are 7 flowers. Sam picks 2.
How many flowers are left?

flower

☐ _____
label

PATH to FLUENCY Subtract.

1 $2 - 2 =$ ☐   **2** $4 - 2 =$ ☐   **3** $4 - 4 =$ ☐

✔ **Check Understanding**
Listen to the story problem.
Draw a Math Mountain or write
an equation to solve the problem.

Solve Mixed Problems

Number Quilt 3: Any Unknown

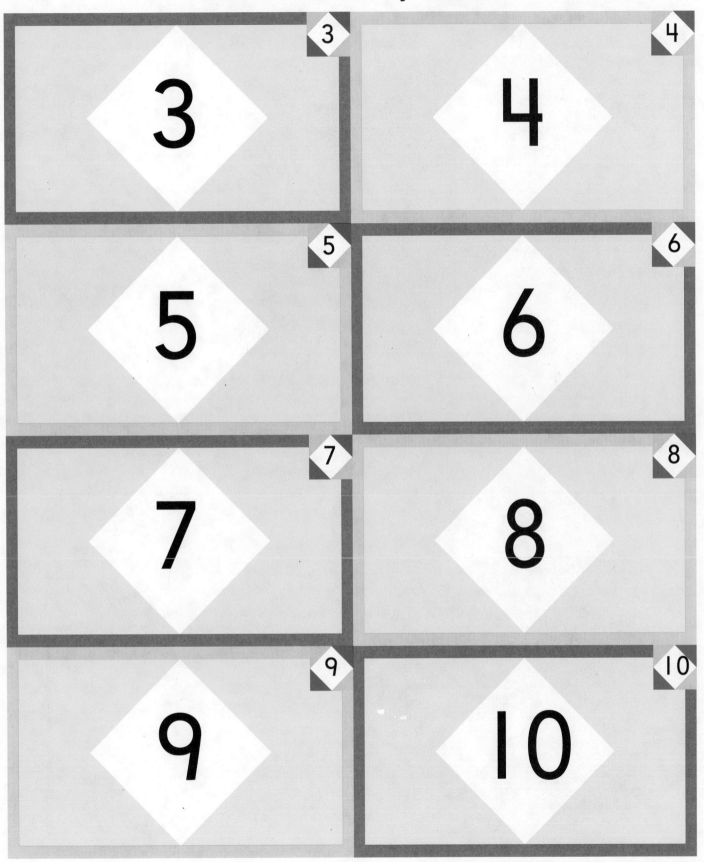

Use with any of the Count-On Cards.

Number Quilt 3

Name _____

Solve the story problem.

1 There are 4 owls in the tree. Then some more owls come. Now there are 6 owls in the tree. How many owls come?

owl

☐ _____
label

2 Some children are on the bus. 5 more get on the bus. Now there are 8. How many children are on the bus before?

bus

☐ _____
label

3 There are 7 plants in the garden. There are 2 carrot plants. The rest are onions. How many plants are onions?

onion

☐ _____
label

4 Some lizards are on a log. Then 3 lizards leave. Now there are 7 lizards. How many lizards are there to start?

lizard

☐ _____
label

CC SS Content Standards **1.0A.A.1, 1.0A.C.6, 1.0A.D.8**
Mathematical Practices **MP6**

Solve.

5

6 3

6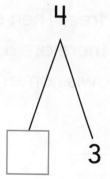

4

3

7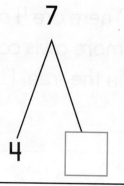

7

4

8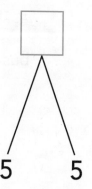

5 5

9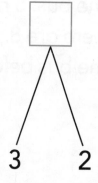

3 2

10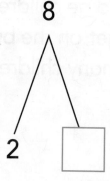

8

2

11

4

3

12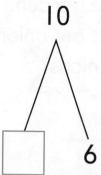

10

6

13

5 2

14 ☐ $+ 8 = 10$ **15** $4 +$ ☐ $= 6$ **16** $10 -$ ☐ $= 2$

✓ Check Understanding

Solve. Draw to show how you solved the equation.

☐ $- 4 = 6$

Practice with Mixed Problems

Name _____

Write the equation to solve.

1 There are 7 balls in the box. Jabar puts some more balls in the box. Now there are 10 balls in the box. How many balls does Jabar put in the box?

   = □

Jabar puts □ balls in the box.

---

2 There were 8 baseballs in the bucket. Leslie takes some baseballs from the bucket. Now there are 6 baseballs in the bucket. How many baseballs does Leslie take?

   = □

Leslie takes □ baseballs.

3 Use the picture to write a story problem.
Write and solve the equation.

_____

- -

_____

_____

- -

_____

_____

- -

_____

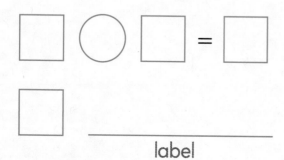

label

Focus on Mathematical Practices

Find the unknown partner or total.
Watch the signs.

1 $6 - 5 = \boxed{}$

2 $8 + 2 = \boxed{}$

3 $7 - \boxed{} = 1$

Solve the story problem.   **Show your work.**

4 Kyle catches 8 frogs.
He lets some frogs go.
Now Kyle has 2 frogs.
How many frogs did he let go?

$\boxed{}$ _____
              label

---

5 Some birds are in a tree. Then 4 birds fly away.
Now there are 5 birds. How many birds
are in the tree at the start?

$\boxed{}$ _____
              label

Subtract.

1 2 − 1 = ☐   **2** 3 − 3 = ☐   **3** 1 − 1 = ☐

4 2 − 2 = ☐   **5** 4 − 2 = ☐   **6** 5 − 5 = ☐

7 7 − 7 = ☐   **8** 6 − 6 = ☐   **9** 6 − 3 = ☐

10 8 − 8 = ☐   **11** 8 − 4 = ☐   **12** 9 − 9 = ☐

13 10 − 10 = ☐   **14** 10 − 5 = ☐   **15** 4 − 4 = ☐

1 Match each set of partners to a total.

6 + 2 = _____ •   • 5

9 − 3 = _____ •   • 10

3 + 7 = _____ •   • 8

8 − 3 = _____ •   • 6

Make three different Math Mountains with a total of 6.

2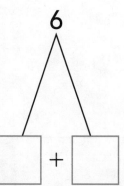
6

☐ + ☐

3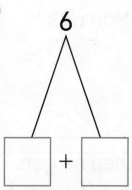
6

☐ + ☐

4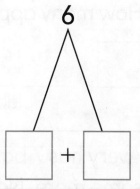
6

☐ + ☐

5 Count on to solve.

8 rakes total

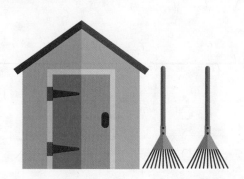

How many rakes are in the shed?

☐ _____
label

Solve the story problem.

6 Maisy has 5 balloons. She gets some more balloons. Now she has 9 balloons. How many balloons does Maisy get?

balloon

☐ _____
label

7 Han picks 5 apples.
Then he picks 3 more.
How many apples does Han pick?

apple

☐ _____
label

8 Avery has 7 baseballs. Then he gets some more. Now Avery has 10 baseballs. How many baseballs does he get?

ball

☐ _____
label

Complete the equations.
Use the numbers on the tiles.

| 6 | 5 | 4 | 8 |

9 $10 - \boxed{} = 2$

10 $4 + \boxed{} = 8$

11 $3 + \boxed{} = 9$

12 $8 - \boxed{} = 3$

Ring the number that makes the sentence true.

13 Lila has 10 books. She gives 4 books away.

book

Now Lila has | 4
6
10 | books.

14 Use the picture to write a story problem.
Write and solve the equation.

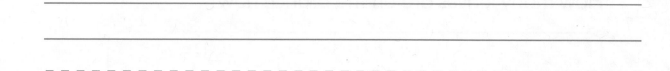

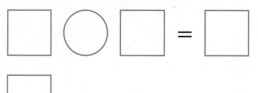
=

label

Solve the story problem.

15 Marty sees 8 birds at a feeder.
There are red birds and blue birds.
How many of each color bird can Marty see?
Show three correct answers.

bird

☐ red birds and ☐ blue birds

or ☐ red birds and ☐ blue birds

or ☐ red birds and ☐ blue birds

16 Read the story problem. Write a subtraction
and an addition equation for the story.
Draw a Math Mountain to match.

There are 7 leaves on the branch.
Then 3 leaves fall off.
How many leaves are on the branch now?

Hide and Seek

Some children are playing hide and seek.

Choose a number from 1–10 for each ☐ .
Use each number only once.

1 10 children are playing. ☐ go and hide.
How many are left?

☐ children

2 ☐ children are hiding. ☐ more children
hide. How many children are hiding?

☐ children

3 Write equations for Problems 1 and 2.

☐ ◯ ☐ = ☐ | ☐ ◯ ☐ = ☐

4 Show you know which partners and total to write in
each equation. Use drawings, numbers, or words.

Soccer

Some children are playing soccer.
Choose a number from 1–10. Use each number only once.

5 **Part A** 10 children play soccer. ☐ players leave.

How many are left? ☐ children

Part B Draw a picture to tell the story.

[ ]

Write an equation for the story.

6 **Part A** 4 children play soccer. ☐ players join.

How many in all? ☐ children

Part B Draw a picture to tell the story.

[ ]

Write an equation for the story.

Dear Family:

Your child is learning about place value and numbers to 100. In this program, children begin by counting tens: 10, 20, 30, 40, and so on. They use a 10 × 10 Grid to help them "see" the relationship between the tens digit in a decade number and the number of tens it has.

10 20 30 40

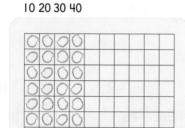

40 is 4 tens.

Soon, children will link 2-digit numbers to tens and extra ones. They will learn that a 2-digit number, such as 46, is made up of tens and ones, such as 40 and 6. Next, children will use what they know about adding 1-digit numbers to add 2-digit numbers.

$$3 + 4 = 7, \text{ so } 30 + 40 = 70.$$

Finally, they will learn to regroup and count on to find a total. For example:

$$19 + 5 = \boxed{24}$$

20
(19) ○ ○ ○ ○ ○ 24

Right now, your child may enjoy counting by tens for you. He or she may also enjoy using household items to make groups of ten and extra ones, and then telling you the total number.

Sincerely,
Your child's teacher

CC SS **Unit 4 addresses the following standards from the** Common Core State Standards for Mathematics: **1.OA.A.1, 1.OA.B.3, 1.OA.C.5, 1.OA.C.6, 1.OA.D.8, 1.NBT.A.1, 1.NBT.B.2, 1.NBT.B.2.a, 1.NBT.B.2.b, 1.NBT.B.2.c, 1.NBT.B.3, 1.NBT.C.4, and all** Mathematical Practices.

Estimada familia:

Su niño está aprendiendo sobre valor posicional y los números hasta 100. En este programa, los niños empiezan contando decenas: 10, 20, 30, 40, etc. Usan una cuadrícula de 10 por 10 como ayuda para "ver" la relación entre el dígito de las decenas en el número que termina en cero y el número de decenas que tiene.

10 20 30 40

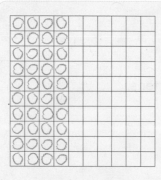

40 es 4 decenas.

En poco tiempo, los niños harán la conexión entre números de 2 dígitos y decenas más otras unidades. Aprenderán que un número de 2 dígitos, tal como 46, consta de decenas y unidades, como 40 y 6. Luego, los niños usarán lo que saben de la suma de números de 1 dígito para sumar números de 2 dígitos.

$$3 + 4 = 7, \text{ por lo tanto } 30 + 40 = 70.$$

Finalmente, aprenderán a reagrupar y contar hacia adelante para hallar el total. Por ejemplo:

$$19 + 5 = \boxed{24}$$

20
⟮19⟯ ○ ○ ○ ○ ○ 24

Por lo pronto, tal vez a su niño le guste contar en decenas para Ud. También puede gustarle usar objetos del hogar para formar grupos de diez más otras unidades y luego decir el número total.

Atentamente,
El maestro de su niño

CC SS **En la Unidad 4 se aplican los siguientes estándares de los** Estándares estatales comunes de matemáticas: **1.OA.A.1, 1.OA.B.3, 1.OA.C.5, 1.OA.C.6, 1.OA.D.8, 1.NBT.A.1, 1.NBT.B.2, 1.NBT.B.2.a, 1.NBT.B.2.b, 1.NBT.B.2.c, 1.NBT.B.3, 1.NBT.C.4 y todos los de** Prácticas matemáticas.

Introduction to Tens Groupings

compare

doubles plus 1

doubles minus 1

doubles plus 2

doubles minus 2

number word

$6 + 6 = 12$, so
$6 + 7 = 13$, 1 more than 12.

11 is less than 12.
$11 < 12$

12 is greater than 11.
$12 > 11$

$6 + 6 = 12$, so
$6 + 8 = 14$, 2 more than 12.

$7 + 7 = 14$, so
$7 + 6 = 13$, 1 less than 14.

12
twelve ◀— **number word**

$7 + 7 = 14$, so
$7 + 5 = 12$, 2 less than 14.

tens

||||| ○○○○○
○

tens

56 has 5 **tens**.

Name _____

How many circles? Count by **tens**.

 1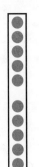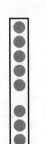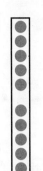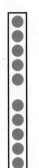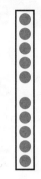

_____ _____ _____ _____ _____ _____ _____

Total _____

Add 1 ten.

 2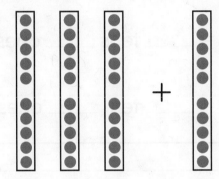

Equation _____

 3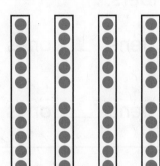

Equation _____

4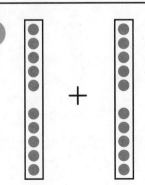

Equation _____

5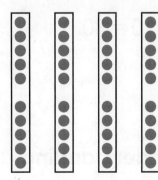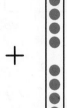

Equation _____

CC SS Content Standards **1.OA.C.5, 1.NBT.A.1, 1.NBT.B.2, 1.NBT.B.2.a, 1.NBT.B.2.c**
Mathematical Practices **MP2, MP3, MP6, MP7**

Introduction to Tens Groupings **145**

Add 10.

6 50 + 10 = ☐

7 10 + 10 = ☐

8 30 + 10 = ☐

9 80 + 10 = ☐

10 70 + 10 = ☐

11 60 + 10 = ☐

12 40 + 10 = ☐

13 90 + 10 = ☐

Write the numbers.

14 20 = _____ tens _____ ones

15 80 = _____ tens _____ ones

16 50 = _____ tens _____ ones

17 10 = _____ ten _____ ones

18 Draw tens to solve.
Write the unknown number.

☐ + 10 = 30

✓ **Check Understanding**
How are counting tens and
adding tens the same?

Introduction to Tens Groupings

Name _____

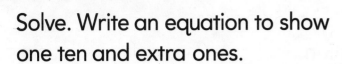

Solve. Write an equation to show one ten and extra ones.

① Choi has 10 pencils in a pack and 4 extra pencils. How many pencils does he have in all?

pencil

[ ] + [ ] = [ ]   [ ] pencils

② There are 10 cups in a box and 7 extra cups. How many cups are there altogether?

cup

[ ] + [ ] = [ ]   [ ] cups

③ Ginger has a tray of 10 plants and 2 extra plants. How many plants are there in all?

plant

[ ] + [ ] = [ ]   [ ] plants

④ Abe has a pail of 10 brushes and 8 extra brushes. How many brushes are there in all?

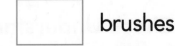

paintbrush

[ ] + [ ] = [ ]   [ ] brushes

© Houghton Mifflin Harcourt Publishing Company

Draw circles in the grid to show
the teen number. Write the equation.

5 Model 16

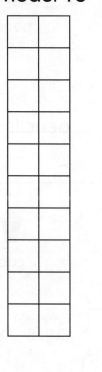

_____ + _____ = _____

6 Model 13

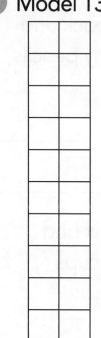

_____ + _____ = _____

7 Model 11

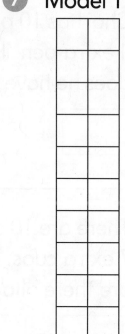

_____ + _____ = _____

8 There is a set of 10 books on a shelf
and 5 extra books. How many books
are there altogether?

Show the teen number in two different ways.

✓ Check Understanding

Explain what a teen number is.

Explore Teen Numbers

© Houghton Mifflin Harcourt Publishing Company

Dear Family:

To help children "see" the tens and ones in 2-digit numbers, the *Math Expressions* program uses special drawings of 10-sticks to show tens, and circles to show ones. These images help children learn place value. Below are the numbers 27 and 52 shown with 10-sticks and circles:

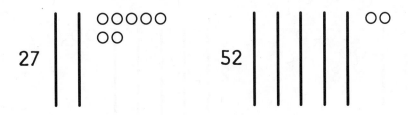

10-sticks and circles will also be used later to help children solve addition problems that require regrouping (sometimes called "carrying"). When there are enough circles to make a new ten, they are circled and then added like a 10-stick. The problem below shows 38 + 5:

Step 1: Show the two numbers with 10-sticks and circles.

$$38 \quad + \quad 5$$

Step 2: Group the ones to make a new ten. Count by tens and ones.

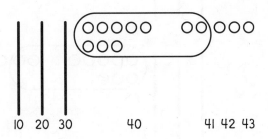

10   20   30   40   41 42 43

Right now, your child is just beginning to show teen numbers with 10-sticks and circles. Soon your child will be able to draw 10-sticks and circles for any 2-digit number.

Sincerely,
Your child's teacher

CC SS Unit 4 addresses the following standards from the Common Core State Standards for Mathematics: **1.OA.A.1, 1.OA.B.3, 1.OA.C.5, 1.OA.C.6, 1.OA.D.8, 1.NBT.A.1, 1.NBT.B.2, 1.NBT.B.2.a, 1.NBT.B.2.b, 1.NBT.B.2.c, 1.NBT.B.3, 1.NBT.C.4,** and all Mathematical Practices.

Estimada familia:

Para ayudar a los niños a "ver" las decenas y las unidades en los números de 2 dígitos, el programa *Math Expressions* usa dibujos especiales de palitos de decenas para mostrar las decenas, y círculos para mostrar las unidades. Estas imágenes ayudan a los niños a aprender el valor posicional. Abajo se muestran los números 27 y 52 con palitos de decenas y círculos:

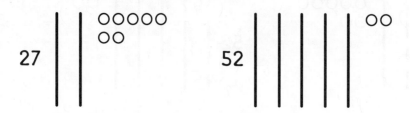

Más adelante, los palitos de decenas y los círculos también se usarán para ayudar a los niños a resolver problemas de suma que requieren reagrupar (que a veces se llama "llevar"). Cuando hay suficientes círculos para formar una nueva decena, se encierran en un círculo y se suman como si fueran un palito de decena. El siguiente problema muestra 38 + 5:

Paso 1: Mostrar los dos números con palitos de decenas y círculos.

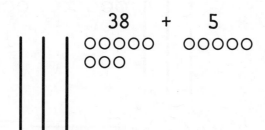

Paso 2: Agrupar las unidades para formar una nueva decena. Contar en decenas y unidades.

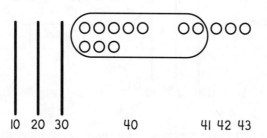

Su niño está comenzando a mostrar los números de 11 a 19 con palitos de decenas y círculos. Pronto, podrá dibujar palitos de decenas y círculos para cualquier número de 2 dígitos.

Atentamente,
El maestro de su niño

CC SS **En la Unidad 4 se aplican los siguientes estándares de los** Estándares estatales comunes de matemáticas: **1.OA.A.1, 1.OA.B.3, 1.OA.C.5, 1.OA.C.6, 1.OA.D.8, 1.NBT.A.1, 1.NBT.B.2, 1.NBT.B.2.a, 1.NBT.B.2.b, 1.NBT.B.2.c, 1.NBT.B.3, 1.NBT.C.4 y todos los de** Prácticas matemáticas.

Represent and Compare Teen Numbers

Name _____

Write the teen number for each model.

1 | ○○○○○

    [ ]

2 | ○○○

    [ ]

3 | ○○○○○
        ○○○

    [ ]

4 | ○○

    [ ]

5 | ○○○○○
        ○○○○

    [ ]

6 | ○○○○

    [ ]

Draw a stick for 10 and circles for ones to represent the teen number.

7 Ben buys a package of 10 erasers. He already has 2 erasers. How many erasers does Ben have now?

[ ]

8 Olivia has 16 bottles of water. A box holds 10. Draw a stick and circles to show how many boxes she can fill and how many bottles will be left over.

[ ]

Write the number. Compare the numbers. Use =, <, or >.

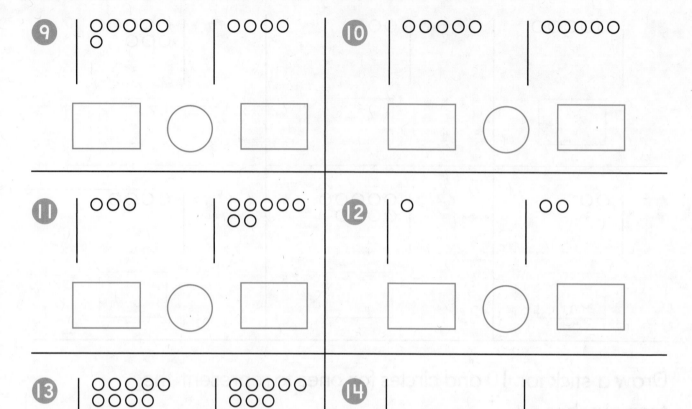

⑮ Compare the numbers 16 and 12 two different ways. Draw to explain.

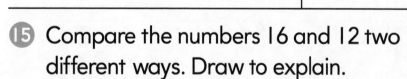

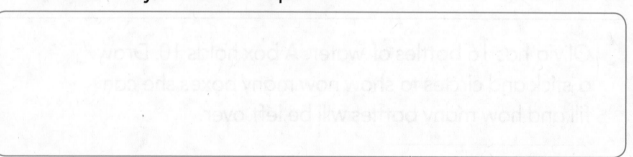

✓ Check Understanding

Draw to explain why 15 is greater than 11.

Represent and Compare Teen Numbers

Name _____

1 Look at what Puzzled Penguin wrote.

$7 + 8 = 10 + \boxed{3}$

$7 + 8 = \boxed{13}$

Am I correct?

2 Help Puzzled Penguin.

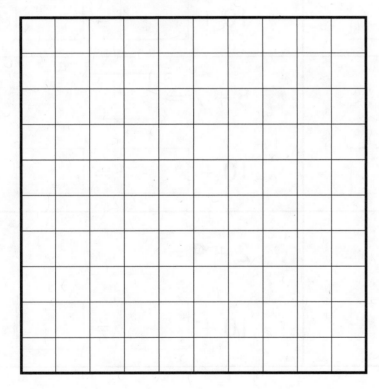

$7 + 8 = 10 + \boxed{}$

$7 + 8 = \boxed{}$

CC SS Content Standards **1.OA.D.8, 1.NBT.B.2.a, 1.NBT.B.2.b**
Mathematical Practices **MP2, MP3, MP6**

Find the total. Then make a ten.

3 $7 + 4 =$ ☐

$10 +$ ☐ $=$ ☐

4 $8 + 8 =$ ☐

$10 +$ ☐ $=$ ☐

5 $8 + 4 =$ ☐

$10 +$ ☐ $=$ ☐

6 $9 + 6 =$ ☐

$10 +$ ☐ $=$ ☐

7 $8 + 6 =$ ☐

$10 +$ ☐ $=$ ☐

8 $5 + 7 =$ ☐

$10 +$ ☐ $=$ ☐

9 $5 + 8 =$ ☐

$10 +$ ☐ $=$ ☐

10 $2 + 9 =$ ☐

$10 +$ ☐ $=$ ☐

11 Write two equations that show different partners for 13. Use 10 in one equation.

_____

_____

✓ Check Understanding

How can $10 + 4$ help you solve $9 + 5$?

Visualize Teen Addition

$5 + 7 = \boxed{}$

$6 + 7 = \boxed{}$

$9 + 9 = \boxed{}$

$8 + 7 = \boxed{}$

$9 + 7 = \boxed{}$

$3 + 8 = \boxed{}$

$4 + 8 = \boxed{}$

$5 + 8 = \boxed{}$

$6 + 8 = \boxed{}$

$7 + 8 = \boxed{}$

$8 + 8 = \boxed{}$

$9 + 8 = \boxed{}$

$3 + 9 = \boxed{}$

$4 + 9 = \boxed{}$

$5 + 9 = \boxed{}$

Green Make-a-Ten Cards **155**

$9 + 9 = \boxed{18}$

9	•	••• •••

9 + 1 + 8

$6 + 7 = \boxed{13}$

7	•••	•••

7 + 3 + 3

$5 + 7 = \boxed{12}$

7	•••	••

7 + 3 + 2

$3 + 8 = \boxed{11}$

8	••	•

8 + 2 + 1

$9 + 7 = \boxed{16}$

9	•	•••••

9 + 1 + 6

$8 + 7 = \boxed{15}$

8	••	•••••

8 + 2 + 5

$6 + 8 = \boxed{14}$

8	••	••••

8 + 2 + 4

$5 + 8 = \boxed{13}$

8	••	•••

8 + 2 + 3

$4 + 8 = \boxed{12}$

8	••	••

8 + 2 + 2

$9 + 8 = \boxed{17}$

9	•	••••

9 + 1 + 7

$8 + 8 = \boxed{16}$

8	••	••••••

8 + 2 + 6

$7 + 8 = \boxed{15}$

8	••	•••••

8 + 2 + 5

$5 + 9 = \boxed{14}$

9	•	••••

9 + 1 + 4

$4 + 9 = \boxed{13}$

9	•	•••

9 + 1 + 3

$3 + 9 = \boxed{12}$

9	•	••

9 + 1 + 2

Green Make-a-Ten Cards

6 + 9 = ☐

7 + 9 = ☐

7 + 4 = ☐

8 + 4 = ☐

9 + 4 = ☐

6 + 5 = ☐

7 + 5 = ☐

8 + 5 = ☐

9 + 5 = ☐

5 + 6 = ☐

8 + 9 = ☐

7 + 6 = ☐

8 + 6 = ☐

9 + 6 = ☐

4 + 7 = ☐

Green Make-a-Ten Cards

7 + 4 = |11|
7 | ••• • |
7 + 3 + 1

7 + 9 = |16|
9 | • ••••• |
9 + 1 + 6

6 + 9 = |15|
9 | • ••••• |
9 + 1 + 5

6 + 5 = |11|
6 | •••• • |
6 + 4 + 1

9 + 4 = |13|
9 | • ••• |
9 + 1 + 3

8 + 4 = |12|
8 | •• •• |
8 + 2 + 2

9 + 5 = |14|
9 | • •••• |
9 + 1 + 4

8 + 5 = |13|
8 | •• ••• |
8 + 2 + 3

7 + 5 = |12|
7 | ••• •• |
7 + 3 + 2

7 + 6 = |13|
7 | ••• ••• |
7 + 3 + 3

8 + 9 = |17|
9 | • •••••• |
9 + 1 + 7

5 + 6 = |11|
6 | •••• • |
6 + 4 + 1

4 + 7 = |11|
7 | ••• • |
7 + 3 + 1

9 + 6 = |15|
9 | • ••••• |
9 + 1 + 5

8 + 6 = |14|
8 | •• •••• |
8 + 2 + 4

Green Make-a-Ten Cards

Name _____

Find the teen total.

1 5 + 9 = [ ]

2 7 + 5 = [ ]

3 7 + 4 = [ ]

4 9 + 6 = [ ]

5 9 + 8 = [ ]

6 9 + 9 = [ ]

7 3 + 9 = [ ]

8 7 + 8 = [ ]

9 9 + 4 = [ ]

10 6 + 5 = [ ]

11 8 + 8 = [ ]

12 8 + 4 = [ ]

13 7 + 6 = [ ]

14 9 + 7 = [ ]

15 Write an equation with a teen total. Draw or explain how making a ten can help you solve your equation.

_____

Find the total.

16 $10 + 9 =$ ☐

17 $9 + 10 =$ ☐

18 $6 + 4 =$ ☐

19 $10 + 3 =$ ☐

20 $10 + 8 =$ ☐

21 $3 + 10 =$ ☐

22 $1 + 9 =$ ☐

23 $10 + 10 =$ ☐

24 Draw or write to explain how you solved Exercise 23.

✓ **Check Understanding**

Explain how to use the Make a Ten strategy to solve $8 + 6$?

Teen Addition Strategies

Name _____

VOCABULARY
doubles plus 1
doubles minus 1
doubles plus 2
doubles minus 2

Use doubles to find the total.

1 5 + 5 = ☐ **2** 6 + 6 = ☐ **3** 7 + 7 = ☐

4 8 + 8 = ☐ **5** 9 + 9 = ☐ **6** 10 + 10 = ☐

Use **doubles plus 1** or **doubles minus 1** to find the total.

7 4 + 4 = 8
  4 + 5 = 8 + ___ = ___

8 8 + 8 = 16
  8 + 7 = 16 − ___ = ___

9 5 + 6 = ☐ **10** 9 + 8 = ☐ **11** 6 + 7 = ☐

Use **doubles plus 2** or **doubles minus 2** to find the total.

12 4 + 4 = 8
  4 + 6 = 8 + ___ = ___

13 8 + 8 = 16
  8 + 6 = 16 − ___ = ___

14 7 + 5 = ☐ **15** 7 + 9 = ☐ **16** 6 + 8 = ☐

Use a double to find the total.

17 8
    + 7

18 10
    + 8

19 5
    + 7

20 6
    + 5

21 8
    + 9

22 7
    + 8

23 7
    + 5

24 7
    + 6

25 Write the double you used to solve Exercise 23.

_____

PATH to FLUENCY Subtract.

1 6
   − 5

2 9
   − 2

3 7
   − 3

4 8
   − 2

5 10
   − 1

6 9
   − 4

7 8
   − 5

8 10
   − 8

 Check Understanding

Write a doubles plus 1 equation for 6 + 6.

_____

Investigate Doubles

Find the total. Then make a ten.

1 7 + 5 = ☐

10 + ☐ = ☐

2 2 + 9 = ☐

10 + ☐ = ☐

Use doubles or doubles plus 1 to find the total.

3 6 + 6 = ☐

4 9 + 8 = ☐

5 8 + 7 = ☐

Name _____ Date _____

Subtract.

1 6
   − 2

2 8
   − 1

3 7
   − 0

4 8
   − 4

5 7
   − 3

6 6
   − 3

7 9
   − 4

8 6
   − 5

9 7
   − 2

10 10
    − 5

11 9
    − 6

12 10
    − 2

13 9
    − 7

14 10
    − 9

15 8
    − 5

Name _____

Write the number.

1

2

3

4

5

6

7

8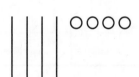

9

10

11

12

Content Standards **1.OA.C.5, 1.NBT.B.2, 1.NBT.B.2.c**
Mathematical Practices **MP2**

Draw 10-sticks and circles. Write the equation.

⑬   32

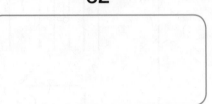

☐ + ☐ = ☐

⑭   68

☐ + ☐ = ☐

⑮   93

☐ + ☐ = ☐

⑯   77

☐ + ☐ = ☐

Draw 10-sticks and circles. Write the number.

⑰   4 tens 8 ones

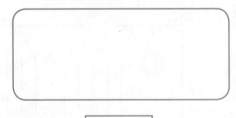

☐

⑱   8 tens 3 ones

☐

✓ Check Understanding

Draw 10-sticks and circles to show 63.
Write the number of tens and ones.

Understand Tens and Ones

Name _____

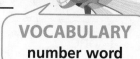

VOCABULARY
number word

1 one	11 eleven	10 ten
2 two	12 twelve	20 twenty
3 three	13 thirteen	30 thirty
4 four	14 fourteen	40 forty
5 five	15 fifteen	50 fifty
6 six	16 sixteen	60 sixty
7 seven	17 seventeen	70 seventy
8 eight	18 eighteen	80 eighty
9 nine	19 nineteen	90 ninety
10 ten	20 twenty	

Write the number.

1 five _____   fifteen _____   fifty _____

2 three _____   thirteen _____   thirty _____

3 two _____   twelve _____   twenty _____

4 sixty _____   sixteen _____   six _____

5 eighteen _____   eighty _____   eight _____

Write the **number word**.

6 4 _____   14 _____   40 _____

7 9 _____   19 _____   90 _____

8 2 _____   12 _____   20 _____

9 1 _____   10 _____   11 _____

1 one	11 eleven	10 ten
2 two	12 twelve	20 twenty
3 three	13 thirteen	30 thirty
4 four	14 fourteen	40 forty
5 five	15 fifteen	50 fifty
6 six	16 sixteen	60 sixty
7 seven	17 seventeen	70 seventy
8 eight	18 eighteen	80 eighty
9 nine	19 nineteen	90 ninety
10 ten	20 twenty	

Write the number word.

10 |○○ _____

11 || _____

12 ||||| _____

13 ○○○○○ _____

14 Write the numbers 1–20.

1									
									20

15 Write the decade numbers 10–90.

10	20							

✓ **Check Understanding**

Explain how the numbers 2, 12, and 20 are the same and how they are different.

Integrate Tens and Ones

Name _____

Draw 10-sticks and circles.
Write the total.

① [ ] = 50 + 3

② [ ] = 70 + 6

③ [ ] = 20 + 9

④ [ ] = 40 + 2

⑤ [ ] = 30 + 7

⑥ [ ] = 10 + 8

⑦ [ ] = 90 + 1

⑧ [ ] = 50 + 5

CC SS Content Standards **1.NBT.A.1, 1.NBT.B.2, 1.NBT.B.2.a, 1.NBT.B.2.c, 1.NBT.C.4**
Mathematical Practices **MP2, MP3, MP6**

Draw 10-sticks and circles to add.
Write the total.

9 || oooo

24 + 3 = ☐

10 || ooooo oo

27 + 6 = ☐

11 ||||| o

41 + 5 = ☐

12 |||||| || ooooo oooo

79 + 5 = ☐

13 |||||| ooooo oo

67 + 2 = ☐

14 |||||| oooo

54 + 4 = ☐

15 |||||| | ooooo

65 + 6 = ☐

16 ||| ooo

33 + 7 = ☐

✔ Check Understanding
Explain how to add 29 + 3.

Practice Grouping Ones into Tens

Name _____

Each box has 10 muffins. How many muffins are there?

① 10 10 10 10 [ ]

② 10 10 [ ]

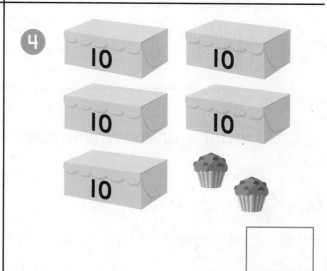

③ 10 [ ]

④ 10 10 10 10 10 [ ]

⑤

10 10 10 10 10 10 10 10 10 [ ]

⑥ How are 23 and 32 the same?
How are they different?

CC SS Content Standards **1.OA.C.6, 1.OA.D.8, 1.NBT.A.1, 1.NBT.B.2, 1.NBT.B.2.b, 1.NBT.C.4**
Mathematical Practices **MP2, MP8**

PATH to FLUENCY Add.

1 $3 + 3 =$ ☐

2 $4 + 5 =$ ☐

3 $1 + 5 =$ ☐

4 $3 + 7 =$ ☐

5 $8 + 0 =$ ☐

6 $2 + 5 =$ ☐

7 ☐ $= 5 + 2$

8 ☐ $= 7 + 1$

9 ☐ $= 5 + 5$

10 ☐ $= 1 + 6$

11 ☐ $= 7 + 3$

12 ☐ $= 5 + 3$

PATH to FLUENCY Find the unknown number.

13 $2 +$ ☐ $= 9$

14 $6 +$ ☐ $= 10$

15 $4 +$ ☐ $= 7$

16 $8 +$ ☐ $= 10$

17 $3 +$ ☐ $= 8$

18 $1 +$ ☐ $= 10$

19 ☐ $+ 3 = 9$

20 ☐ $+ 6 = 8$

21 ☐ $+ 8 = 9$

22 ☐ $+ 6 = 6$

23 ☐ $+ 4 = 7$

24 ☐ $+ 2 = 9$

✓ **Check Understanding**

Explain how to use tens and ones to find $43 + 6$.

Add with Groups of Ten

1	2	10	20
1	**2**	**1 0**	**2 0**

3	4	30	40
3	**4**	**3 0**	**4 0**

5	6	50	60
5	**6**	**5 0**	**6 0**

7	8	70	80
7	**8**	**7 0**	**8 0**

9	90	100
9	**9 0**	**1 0 0**

Secret Code Cards

Name _____

Write the number of tens and ones.
Write the number.

1

___ tens ___ ones

2

___ tens ___ ones

3

___ tens ___ ones

4

___ tens ___ ones

5

___ tens ___ ones

6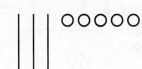

___ tens ___ ones

7

___ tens ___ ones

8

___ tens ___ ones

Content Standards **1.NBT.A.1, 1.NBT.B.2, 1.NBT.C.4**
Mathematical Practices **MP2**

Practice with Tens and Ones **175**

Draw 10-sticks and circles.
Write the number of tens and ones.

9　　75

_____ tens _____ ones

10　　90

_____ tens _____ ones

11　　41

_____ tens _____ ones

12　　59

_____ tens _____ ones

13　　26

_____ tens _____ ones

14　　88

_____ tens _____ ones

✓ **Check Understanding**

Draw 10-sticks and circles for a 2-digit number that has 7 tens and another 2-digit number that has 7 ones.

Practice with Tens and Ones

Name _____

VOCABULARY
compare

Compare the numbers. Write >, <, or =.

1.   30 ◯ 25

2.   23 ◯ 28

3. 70 ◯ 80   4. 60 ◯ 59   5. 76 ◯ 67

6. 24 ◯ 84   7. 37 ◯ 37   8. 48 ◯ 50

9. 56 ◯ 56   10. 17 ◯ 42   11. 99 ◯ 33

Compare the numbers two ways.
Write the numbers.

12. Compare 53 and 54.

◯

_____   _____

◯

_____

13. Compare 80 and 79.

◯

_____   _____

◯

_____

14. Compare 49 and 94.

◯

_____   _____

◯

_____

15. Compare 36 and 32.

◯

_____   _____

◯

_____

Content Standards 1.NBT.B.2, 1.NBT.B.3
Mathematical Practices MP2, MP3, MP6

Use Place Value to Compare Numbers **177**

Write to compare the numbers.

16 Compare 39 and 40.

◯

_____   _____

17 Compare 86 and 68.

◯

_____   _____

18 Compare 95 and 91.

◯

_____   _____

19 Compare 72 and 72.

◯

_____   _____

20 Compare 20 and 10.

◯

_____   _____

21 Compare 60 and 16.

◯

_____   _____

22 Look at what Puzzled Penguin wrote.

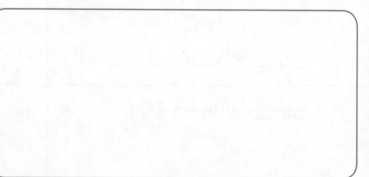

29 (>) 36

Am I correct?

23 Help Puzzled Penguin.

29 ◯ 36

✔ **Check Understanding**
Compare 26 and 62.   _____ ◯ _____

Use Place Value to Compare Numbers

Write the numbers.

1

_____ tens _____ ones = _____

2

_____ tens _____ ones = _____

Compare the numbers. Write >, <, or =.

3 63 ◯ 73

4 42 ◯ 24

5 20 ◯ 20

Name _____ Date _____

Find the unknown partner or total.

1 $3 + 3 = \boxed{}$ 2 $2 + 4 = \boxed{}$ 3 $5 + 3 = \boxed{}$

4 $3 + 4 = \boxed{}$ 5 $8 + 1 = \boxed{}$ 6 $2 + 5 = \boxed{}$

7 $4 + \boxed{} = 6$ 8 $7 + \boxed{} = 9$ 9 $1 + \boxed{} = 7$

10 $4 + \boxed{} = 8$ 11 $8 + \boxed{} = 10$

12 $3 + \boxed{} = 10$ 13 $\boxed{} + 3 = 9$

14 $\boxed{} + 5 = 8$ 15 $\boxed{} + 4 = 10$

Name _____

Write the totals.

1. $4 + 4 =$ ☐

   $40 + 40 =$ ☐

2. $6 + 3 =$ ☐

   $60 + 30 =$ ☐

3. $2 + 3 =$ ☐

   $20 + 30 =$ ☐

4. $1 + 7 =$ ☐

   $10 + 70 =$ ☐

5. $5 + 2 =$ ☐

   $50 + 20 =$ ☐

6. $3 + 3 =$ ☐

   $30 + 30 =$ ☐

7. $7 + 2 =$ ☐

   $70 + 20 =$ ☐

8. $2 + 2 =$ ☐

   $20 + 20 =$ ☐

9. Use 10-sticks and circles to solve.

   $4 + 5 =$ ☐ $40 + 50 =$ ☐

   Explain how the totals are different.

   -

   _____

   _____

   -

   _____

Complete the equation.
Draw a 10-stick or a circle to solve for the total.

10 14

○○○○

☐ + 1 = ☐

11 16

○○○○○
○

☐ + 10 = ☐

12 13

○○○

☐ + 1 = ☐

13 23

○○○

☐ + 1 = ☐

14 39

○○○○○
○○○○

☐ + 10 = ☐

15 42

○○

☐ + 10 = ☐

16 57

○○○○○
○○

☐ + 1 = ☐

 Check Understanding
Explain if the total of
58 + 10 will be 59 or 68.

Add Tens or Ones

Name _____

Solve.

1. $3 + 6 =$ _____
   $30 + 60 =$ _____
   $30 + 6 =$ _____

2. $4 + 5 =$ _____
   $40 + 50 =$ _____
   $40 + 5 =$ _____

3. $2 + 4 =$ _____
   $20 + 40 =$ _____
   $20 + 4 =$ _____

4. $5 + 2 =$ _____
   $50 + 20 =$ _____
   $50 + 2 =$ _____

5. $7 + 2 =$ _____
   $70 + 20 =$ _____
   $70 + 2 =$ _____

6. $4 + 1 =$ _____
   $40 + 10 =$ _____
   $40 + 1 =$ _____

7. $3 + 2 =$ _____
   $30 + 20 =$ _____
   $30 + 2 =$ _____

8. $1 + 8 =$ _____
   $10 + 80 =$ _____
   $10 + 8 =$ _____

Complete the set of equations to follow the same rules as each set above. Then solve.

9. $3 + 5 =$ _____
   $30 +$ _____ $=$ _____
   $30 +$ _____ $=$ _____

10. $4 + 3 =$ _____
    $40 +$ _____ $=$ _____
    $40 +$ _____ $=$ _____

CC SS **Content Standards** 1.OA.D.8, 1.NBT.B.2, 1.NBT.B.2.c, 1.NBT.C.4
Mathematical Practices MP2, MP3, MP6

Find the unknown numbers to complete
the set of equations.

11. 2 + _____ = 5

20 + 30 = _____

20 + _____ = 23

12. 4 + _____ = 8

_____ + 40 = 80

40 + 4 = _____

13. _____ + 2 = 6

40 + _____ = 60

_____ + 2 = 42

14. _____ + 7 = 8

10 + _____ = 80

10 + 7 = _____

15. Look at what Puzzled Penguin wrote.

50 + 4 = | 90 |

Am I correct?

16. Help Puzzled Penguin.

50 + 4 = [ ]

✓ **Check Understanding**

Write tens, ones, or both to add the numbers.

40 + 30   adding _____   40 + 3   adding _____

Mixed Addition with Tens and Ones

Here is a riddle.

> I like to hop,
> but my ears are small.
> I have four legs, but I stand tall.
> I have a pocket,
> but I cannot buy.
> Guess my name. Who am I?

Find the total. Use any method.

① 46 + 5 = [ ]   O   ② 40 + 2 = [ ]   O

③ 12 + 7 = [ ]   K   ④ 29 + 5 = [ ]   R

⑤ 64 + 6 = [ ]   A   ⑥ 20 + 9 = [ ]   A

⑦ 27 + 5 = [ ]   G   ⑧ 89 + 2 = [ ]   N

Who am I? Write the letter for each total.

___ ___ ___ ___ ___ ___ ___ ___
19   70   91   32   29   34   42   51

© Houghton Mifflin Harcourt Publishing Company

PATH to FLUENCY **Add.**

1. $4 + 5 =$ ☐

2. $0 + 7 =$ ☐

3. $7 + 3 =$ ☐

4. $1 + 6 =$ ☐

5. $6 + 2 =$ ☐

6. $4 + 2 =$ ☐

7. ☐ $= 7 + 1$

8. ☐ $= 3 + 6$

9. ☐ $= 7 + 2$

10. ☐ $= 6 + 4$

11. ☐ $= 2 + 4$

12. ☐ $= 4 + 3$

PATH to FLUENCY **Find the unknown number.**

13. $1 +$ ☐ $= 8$

14. $3 +$ ☐ $= 7$

15. $5 +$ ☐ $= 8$

16. $8 +$ ☐ $= 10$

17. $4 +$ ☐ $= 8$

18. $9 +$ ☐ $= 9$

19. ☐ $+ 1 = 6$

20. ☐ $+ 4 = 9$

21. ☐ $+ 7 = 10$

22. ☐ $+ 8 = 9$

23. ☐ $+ 5 = 8$

24. ☐ $+ 8 = 10$

 Check Understanding

Explain how to count on to find $28 + 3$.

Counting On Strategy: 2-Digit Numbers

Use this sandwich sheet when you play
The Sandwich Game.

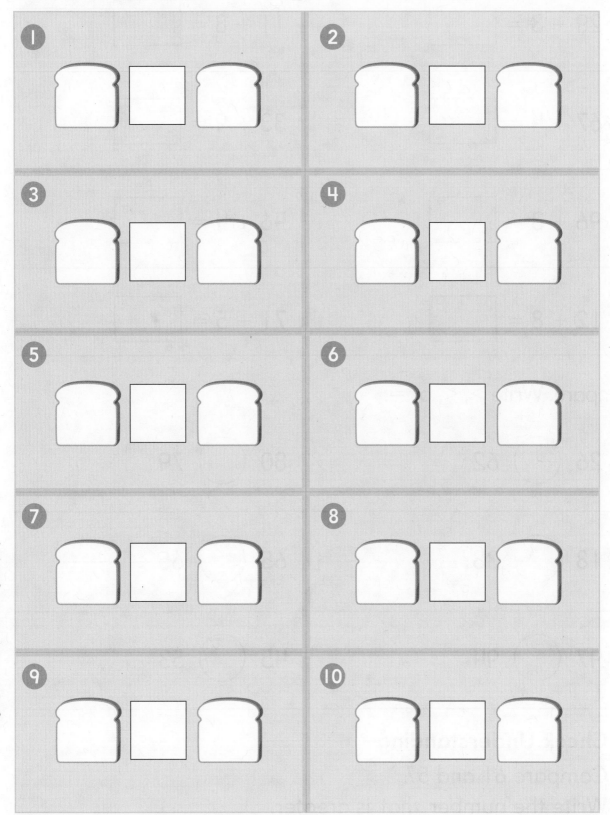

Find the total. Use any method.

11 29 + 3 = ☐   **12** 11 + 8 = ☐

13 67 + 4 = ☐   **14** 33 + 9 = ☐

15 96 + 3 = ☐   **16** 46 + 4 = ☐

17 12 + 8 = ☐   **18** 71 + 5 = ☐

Compare. Write >, <, or =.

19 26 ◯ 62   **20** 80 ◯ 79

21 18 ◯ 38   **22** 65 ◯ 65

23 97 ◯ 94   **24** 45 ◯ 53

 Check Understanding

Compare 61 and 57.

Write the number that is greater. _____

Practice with 2-Digit Numbers

Name _____

Write the number.

 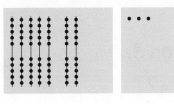

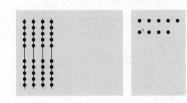

Draw 10-sticks and circles to show the number.

⑤
50 2
5 **2**

⑥
90 7
9 **7**

⑦
60 5
6 **5**

⑧
80 9
8 **9**

Draw 10-sticks and circles to count on.
Write the total.

9 Count on 4.

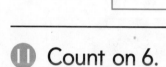

10 Count on 3.

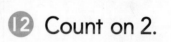

11 Count on 6.

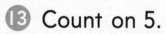

12 Count on 2.

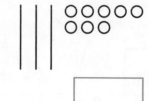

13 Count on 5.

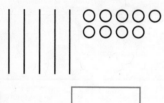

14 Count on 4.

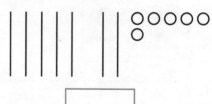

15 Count on 6.

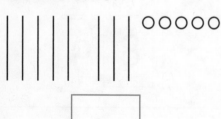

16 Count on 4.

✓ **Check Understanding**

Write the total for 38 + 4.

2-Digit Addition Games

Name _____

Linda and her family go to a show.

1 10 cars can park in each row.

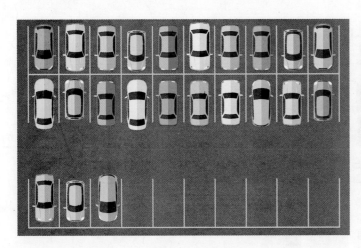

How many cars are there?

_____ tens _____ ones = _____ cars

_____

2 10 people can sit in each row.

How many people are there?

_____ tens _____ ones = _____ people

Show tickets were sold on Friday,
Saturday, and Sunday.

3 Write the number of tickets sold each day.

Friday	
	_____ tens _____ ones = _____ tickets
Saturday	
	_____ tens _____ ones = _____ tickets
Sunday	
	_____ tens _____ ones = _____ tickets

Compare the number of tickets sold.
Use >, <, or =.

4 Friday   Saturday

▢ ◯ ▢

5 Friday   Sunday

▢ ◯ ▢

6 Saturday   Sunday

▢ ◯ ▢

7 Sunday   Saturday

▢ ◯ ▢

Focus on Mathematical Practices

Add.

1 20 + 50 = ⬜

_____

2 60 + 3 = ⬜

_____

Find the total.

3 44 + 3 = ⬜

_____

4 72 + 9 = ⬜

_____

Solve the story problem.   Show your work.

5 Cindy has 56 stamps.
She buys 4 more stamps.
How many stamps does she have now?

⬜ _____
          label

Name _____ Date _____

PATH to
FLUENCY

Find the unknown partner or total.

1 5 + 2 = ☐   **2** 1 + 5 = ☐   **3** 2 + 4 = ☐

4 5 + 4 = ☐   **5** 2 + 6 = ☐   **6** 5 + 5 = ☐

7 1 + ☐ = 7   **8** 4 + ☐ = 6   **9** 0 + ☐ = 8

10 6 + ☐ = 9   **11** 2 + ☐ = 8

12 9 + ☐ = 10   **13** ☐ + 3 = 6

14 ☐ + 0 = 9   **15** ☐ + 7 = 8

1 Does the number match the picture?
Choose Yes or No.

| | | | | 50   ○ Yes   ○ No

| ○ ○ ○   31   ○ Yes   ○ No

Draw 10-sticks and circles.
Write the number of tens and ones.

2   32

[ ] tens [ ] ones = 32

3   64

[ ] tens [ ] ones = 64

Use the words on the tiles to name each number.

| seventy | seven | seventeen |

4 17 _____

5 70 _____

6 7 _____

7 Add 1 ten.

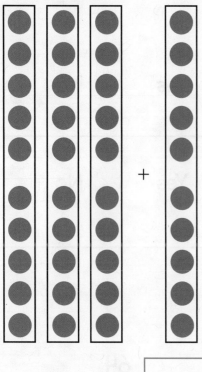

$+$

$30 + 10 =$ ☐

8 How many paper clips?

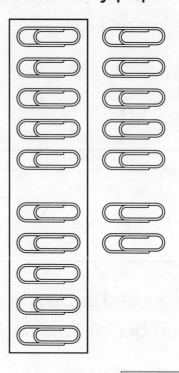

☐

9 Draw a picture for the problem.
Write an equation to solve.

There are 10 birds in one tree.
There are 7 birds in another tree.
How many birds are there?

☐ _____
label

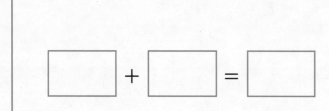

☐ $+$ ☐ $=$ ☐

How many muffins are there?

10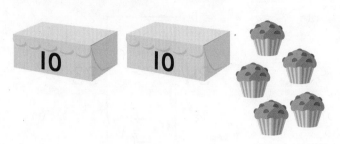

○ 22
○ 25
○ 42
○ 62

11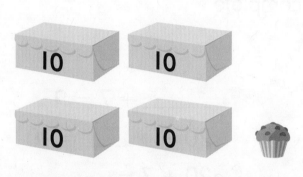

○ 14
○ 29
○ 31
○ 41

Solve the story problem.

12 Kimi has 8 red apples and
5 green apples. How many
apples does she have?

apple

☐

_____
label

13 Hector has a box of 4 red pencils
and 7 blue pencils. How many
pencils does he have?

box

☐

_____
label

Ring >, <, or = to compare the numbers.

⑭ 42 | > < = | 50

⑮ 34 | > < = | 33

Find the unknown numbers to complete
the set of equations.

⑯ 3 + _____ = 7

30 + 40 = _____

30 + _____ = 34

⑰ _____ + 7 = 9

20 + _____ = 90

20 + 7 = _____

⑱ Write a number from 10 to 40.
Add 1 ten. Write the new number.
Draw and write to compare the numbers.

Snack Time

It is snack time at sports camp. Each team gets these drinks.

Water	Milk	Orange Juice	Apple Juice
13 bottles	11 cartons	9 boxes	7 boxes

1 Does each team get more bottles of water or more

cartons of milk? _____

Draw or write to tell how you know.

```

```

2 Draw 10-sticks and circles to show
the number of water bottles.

```

```

3 Each team has 20 children. Does a team get enough juice

boxes for everyone? _____

Draw or write to tell how you know.

```

```

Snack Time (continued)

Use the drink chart on page 199 for Problem 4.

4 **Part A**
The Red team has 20 children.
They choose two kinds of drinks.
Show how many they might
choose of each.

Kind of Drink	How many?

Draw or write to tell how you know there
are 20 drinks.

Part B
The Blue team has 20 children.
No children want milk.
Show how they might choose
other drinks.
(Choose at least one of each).

Kind of Drink	How many?

Draw or write to tell how you know there
are 20 drinks.

Addition and Subtraction Problem Types

	Result Unknown	Change Unknown	Start Unknown
Add To	Six children are playing tag in the yard. Three more children come to play. How many children are playing in the yard now? *Situation and Solution Equation[1]:* $6 + 3 = \square$	Six children are playing tag in the yard. Some more children come to play. Now there are 9 children in the yard. How many children came to play? *Situation Equation:* $6 + \square = 9$ *Solution Equation:* $9 - 6 = \square$	Some children are playing tag in the yard. Three more children come to play. Now there are 9 children in the yard. How many children were in the yard at first? *Situation Equation:* $\square + 3 = 9$ *Solution Equation:* $9 - 3 = \square$
Take From	Jake has 10 trading cards. He gives 3 to his brother. How many trading cards does he have left? *Situation and Solution Equation:* $10 - 3 = \square$	Jake has 10 trading cards. He gives some to his brother. Now Jake has 7 trading cards left. How many cards does he give to his brother? *Situation Equation:* $10 - \square = 7$ *Solution Equation:* $10 - 7 = \square$	Jake has some trading cards. He gives 3 to his brother. Now Jake has 7 trading cards left. How many cards does he start with? *Situation Equation:* $\square - 3 = 7$ *Solution Equation:* $7 + 3 = \square$

[1]A situation equation represents the structure (action) in the problem situation. A solution equation shows the operation used to find the answer.

Problem Types

Addition and Subtraction Problem Types (continued)

	Total Unknown	Addend Unknown	Other Addend Unknown
Put Together/ Take Apart	There are 9 red roses and 4 yellow roses in a vase. How many roses are in the vase? *Math Drawing²:* □ 9　4 *Situation and Solution Equation:* $9 + 4 = \square$	Thirteen roses are in the vase. 9 are red and the rest are yellow. How many roses are yellow? *Math Drawing:* 13 9　□ *Situation Equation:* $13 = 9 + \square$ *Solution Equation:* $13 - 9 = \square$	Ana has 13 roses. Some are yellow and 9 are red. How many are yellow? *Math Drawing:* 13 □　9 *Situation Equation:* $13 = \square + 9$ *Solution Equation:* $\square = 13 - 9$

Both Addends Unknown is a productive extension of this basic situation, especially for small numbers less than or equal to 10. Such take apart situations can be used to show all the decompositions of a given number. The associated equations, which have a total on the left of the equal sign, help children understand that the = sign does not always mean makes or results in but always does mean *is the same number as.*

Both Addends Unknown

Ana has 13 roses. How many can she put in her red vase and how many in her blue vase?

Math Drawing:

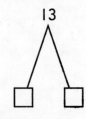

Situation Equation:
$13 = \square + \square$

²These math drawings are called Math Mountains in Grades 1–3 and break-apart drawings in Grades 4 and 5.

Addition and Subtraction Problem Types (continued)

Compare[3]	Difference Unknown	Bigger Unknown	Smaller Unknown
	Aki has 8 apples. Sofia has 14 apples. How many more apples does Sofia have than Aki?	**Leading Language** Aki has 8 apples. Sofia has 6 more apples than Aki. How many apples does Sofia have?	**Leading Language** Sofia has 14 apples. Aki has 6 fewer apples than Sofia. How many apples does Aki have?
	Aki has 8 apples. Sofia has 14 apples. How many fewer apples does Aki have than Sofia?	**Misleading Language** Aki has 8 apples. Aki has 6 fewer apples than Sofia. How many apples does Sofia have?	**Misleading Language** Sofia has 14 apples. Sofia has 6 more apples than Aki. How many apples does Aki have?
	Math Drawing: S [14] A [8] [?] *Situation Equation:* $8 + \square = 14$ *Solution Equation:* $14 - 8 = \square$	*Math Drawing:* S [?] A [8] [6] *Situation and Solution Equation:* $8 + 6 = \square$	*Math Drawing:* S [14] A [?] [6] *Situation Equation:* $\square + 6 = 14$ *Solution Equation:* $14 - 6 = \square$

[3]A comparison sentence can always be said in two ways. One way uses *more*, and the other uses *fewer* or *less*. Misleading language suggests the wrong operation. For example, it says *Aki has 6 fewer apples than Sofia*, but you have to add 6 to Aki's 8 apples to get 14 apples.

Glossary

5-group*

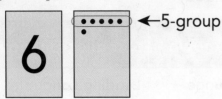 ←5-group

10-group

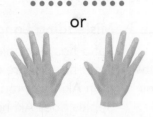

or

10-stick*

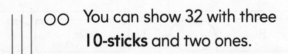 You can show 32 with three **10-sticks** and two ones.

add

3 + 2 = 5
●●● ●●

addend

5 + 4 = 9   5 + 4 + 8 = 17

↑   ↑   ↑   ↑   ↑

addends   addends
(partners)

addition story problem

There are 5 ducks.
Then 3 more come.
How many ducks are there now?

break-apart*

You can **break apart** the number 4.

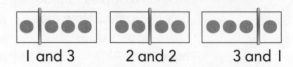

1 and 3   2 and 2   3 and 1

1 and 3, 2 and 2, and 3 and 1 are
break-aparts of 4.

circle

○ ○ ○

circle drawing*

clock

analog
clock

digital
clock

*A classroom research-based term developed for *Math Expressions*

column

1	11	21	31	41	51	61	71	81	91
2	12	22	32	42	52	62	72	82	92
3	13	23	33	43	53	63	73	83	93
4	14	24	34	44	54	64	74	84	94
5	15	25	35	45	55	65	75	85	95
6	16	26	36	46	56	66	76	86	96
7	17	27	37	47	57	67	77	87	97
8	18	28	38	48	58	68	78	88	98
9	19	29	39	49	59	69	79	89	99
10	20	30	40	50	60	70	80	90	100

compare

You can **compare** numbers.

11 is less than 12.

$11 < 12$

12 is greater than 11.

$12 > 11$

You can **compare** objects by length.

The crayon is shorter than the pencil.

The pencil is longer than the crayon.

comparison bars*

Joe has 6 roses. Sasha has 9 roses. How many more roses does Sasha have than Joe?

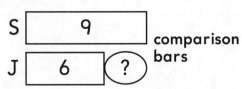

comparison bars

cone

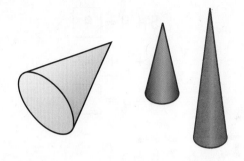

corner

corner

count

count all

$5 + 4 = \boxed{9}$

1 2 3 4 5   6 7 8 9

*A classroom research-based term developed for *Math Expressions*

Glossary

count on

$$5 + 4 = \boxed{9}$$
$$5 + \boxed{4} = 9$$
$$9 - 5 = \boxed{4}$$

5 · · · ·
6 7 8 9

Count on from 5 to get the answer.

cube

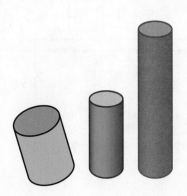

cylinder

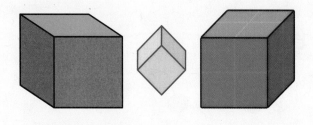

data

Colors in the Bag							
Red	○	○	○				
Yellow	○	○	○	○	○	○	○	○
Blue	○	○	○	○	○	○		

The **data** show how many of each color.

decade numbers

10, 20, 30, 40, 50, 60, 70, 80, 90

difference

$$11 - 3 = 8$$

difference →

$$\begin{array}{r} 11 \\ -\ 3 \\ \hline 8 \end{array}$$

digit

15 is a 2-**digit** number.

The 1 in 15 means 1 ten.

The 5 in 15 means 5 ones.

Dot Array

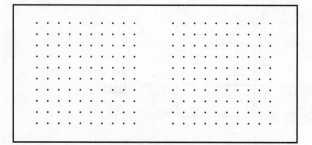

*A classroom research-based term developed for *Math Expressions*

doubles

$$4 + 4 = 8$$

Both partners are the same.
They are doubles.

doubles minus 1

$7 + 7 = 14$, so
$7 + 6 = 13$, 1 less than 14.

doubles minus 2

$7 + 7 = 14$, so
$7 + 5 = 12$, 2 less than 14.

doubles plus 1

$6 + 6 = 12$, so
$6 + 7 = 13$, 1 more than 12.

doubles plus 2

$6 + 6 = 12$, so
$6 + 8 = 14$, 2 more than 12.

E

edge

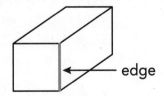

edge

equal shares

2 equal shares   4 equal shares

These show **equal shares.**

equal to (=)

$$4 + 4 = 8$$

4 plus 4 is **equal to** 8.

equation

Examples:

$4 + 3 = 7$ $7 = 4 + 3$

$9 - 5 = 4$ $4 = 9 - 5$

F

face

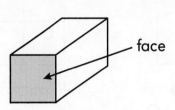

face

fewer

Eggs Laid This Month

Clucker laid **fewer** eggs than Vanilla.

Glossary

fewest

Eggs Laid This Month

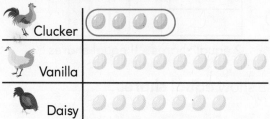

Clucker laid the **fewest** eggs.

fourth of

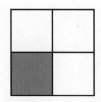

One **fourth of** the shape is shaded.

fourths

 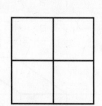

I whole   4 **fourths**, or 4 quarters

greater than (>)

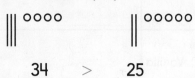

34   >   25

34 is **greater than** 25.

grid

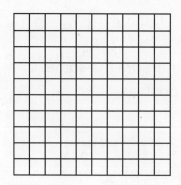

half-hour

A **half-hour** is 30 minutes.

half of

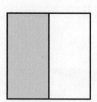

One **half of** the shape is shaded.

halves

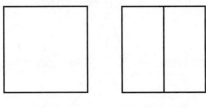

1 whole	2 **halves**

hexagon

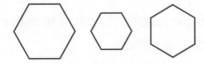

hour

An **hour** is 60 minutes.

hour hand

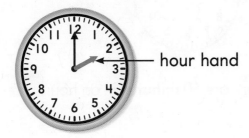

hour hand

hundred

1	11	21	31	41	51	61	71	81	91
2	12	22	32	42	52	62	72	82	92
3	13	23	33	43	53	63	73	83	93
4	14	24	34	44	54	64	74	84	94
5	15	25	35	45	55	65	75	85	95
6	16	26	36	46	56	66	76	86	96
7	17	27	37	47	57	67	77	87	97
8	18	28	38	48	58	68	78	88	98
9	19	29	39	49	59	69	79	89	99
10	20	30	40	50	60	70	80	90	100

or

K

known partner*

$5 + \boxed{} = 7$

5 is the **known partner**.

L

length

The **length** of this pencil is 6 paper clips.

*A classroom research-based term developed for *Math Expressions*

less than (<)

45 < 46

45 is **less than** 46.

longer

The pencil is **longer** than the crayon.

longest

The pencil is the **longest**.

M

make a ten

$8 + 6 = \square$

$8\,\bigcirc\bigcirc\;\bigcirc\bigcirc\bigcirc\bigcirc$

$10 + 4 = 14$,
so $8 + 6 = 14$.

Math Mountain*

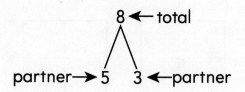

8 ← total

partner → 5   3 ← partner

measure

You can use paper clips to **measure** the length of the pencil.

minus (−)

$$8 - 3 = 5 \qquad \begin{array}{r} 8 \\ -3 \\ \hline 5 \end{array}$$

8 **minus** 3 equals 5.

minute

1 minute

minute hand

There are 60 **minutes** in an hour.

*A classroom research-based term developed for *Math Expressions*

more

Eggs Laid This Month

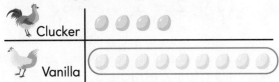

Vanilla laid **more** eggs than Clucker.

most

Eggs Laid This Month

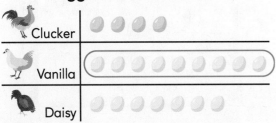

Vanilla laid the **most** eggs.

N

New Group Above Method*

$$\overset{1}{56}$$
$$+\ 28$$
$$\overline{84}$$

$6 + 8 = 14$

The 1 new ten in 14 goes up to the tens place.

New Group Below Method*

$$56$$
$$+\ 28$$
$$\overline{84}$$

$6 + 8 = 14$

The 1 new ten in 14 goes below in the tens place.

not equal to (≠)

$$6 \ne 8$$

6 is **not equal to** 8.

number word

12

twelve ⟵ number word

O

ones

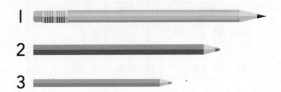
ones

56 has 6 **ones**.

order

You can change the **order** of the partners.

$$7 + 2 = 9$$
$$2 + 7 = 9$$

You can **order** objects by length.

1
2
3

*A classroom research-based term developed for *Math Expressions*

Glossary

partner*

$$5 = 2 + 3$$

2 and 3 are **partners** of 5.
2 and 3 are 5-**partners**.

partner house*

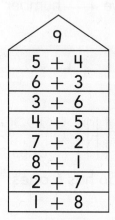

```
        9
      5 + 4
      6 + 3
      3 + 6
      4 + 5
      7 + 2
      8 + 1
      2 + 7
      1 + 8
```

partner train*

4-train

| 3 + 1 | 2 + 2 | 1 + 3 |

pattern

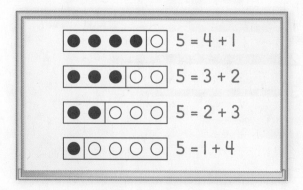

●●●●○ 5 = 4 + 1
●●●○○ 5 = 3 + 2
●●○○○ 5 = 2 + 3
●○○○○ 5 = 1 + 4

The partners of a number show a **pattern**.

plus (+)

$$3 + 2 = 5 \qquad \begin{array}{r} 3 \\ +\ 2 \\ \hline 5 \end{array}$$

3 **plus** 2 equals 5.

Proof Drawing*

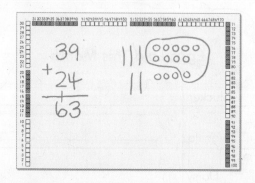

quarter of

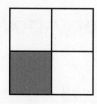

One **quarter of** the shape is shaded.

quarters

1 whole

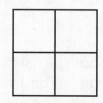

4 quarters, or 4 fourths

*A classroom research-based term developed for *Math Expressions*

R

rectangle

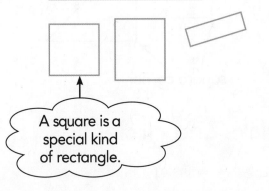

A square is a special kind of rectangle.

rectangular prism

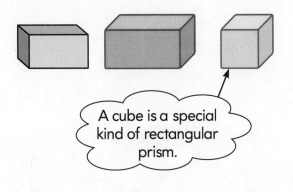

A cube is a special kind of rectangular prism.

row

1	11	21	31	41	51	61	71	81	91
2	12	22	32	42	52	62	72	82	92
3	13	23	33	43	53	63	73	83	93
4	14	24	34	44	54	64	74	84	94
5	15	25	35	45	55	65	75	85	95
6	16	26	36	46	56	66	76	86	96
7	17	27	37	47	57	67	77	87	97
8	18	28	38	48	58	68	78	88	98
9	19	29	39	49	59	69	79	89	99
10	20	30	40	50	60	70	80	90	100

S

shapes

2-dimensional

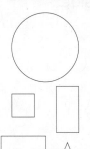

3-dimensional

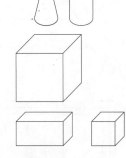

shorter

The crayon is **shorter** than the pencil.

shortest

The paper clip is the **shortest**.

Show All Totals Method*

$$\begin{array}{r} 25 \\ +\ 48 \\ \hline 60 \\ 13 \\ \hline 73 \end{array}$$

*A classroom research-based term developed for *Math Expressions*

side

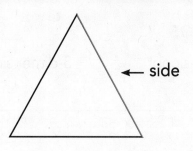

← side

sort

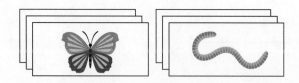

You can **sort** the animals into groups.

sphere

square

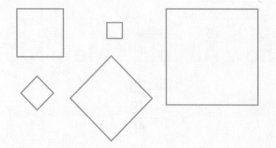

square corner

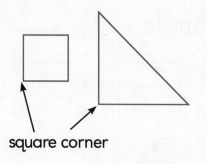

square corner

sticks and circles*

subtract

$$8 - 3 = 5$$

⬤⬤⬤⬤⬤ ⬤⬤⬤

subtraction story problem

8 flies are on a log.
6 are eaten by a frog.
How many flies are left?

*A classroom research-based term developed for *Math Expressions*

switch the partners*

 7 + 2

 2 + 7

T

teen number

11 12 13 14 15 16 17 18 19

teen numbers

teen total*

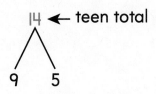

14 ← teen total

9   5

tens

tens

56 has 5 **tens**.

total

4 + 3 = 7

        ↑
   total →

$$\begin{array}{r} 4 \\ + 3 \\ \hline 7 \end{array}$$

trapezoid

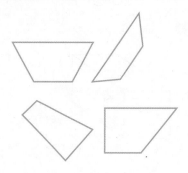

triangle

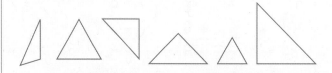

U

unknown partner*

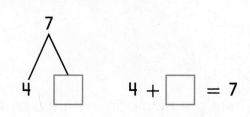

7

4 □   4 + □ = 7

unknown total*

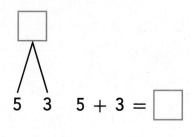

□

5 3   5 + 3 = □

*A classroom research-based term developed for *Math Expressions*

V

vertex

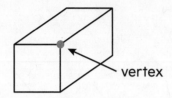

vertex

vertical form

$$\begin{array}{r} 6 \\ +3 \\ \hline 9 \end{array} \qquad \begin{array}{r} 9 \\ -3 \\ \hline 6 \end{array}$$

Z

zero

There are **zero** apples on the plate.

1.OA Operations and Algebraic Thinking

Represent and solve problems involving addition and subtraction.

1.OA.A.1	Use addition and subtraction within 20 to solve word problems involving situations of adding to, taking from, putting together, taking apart, and comparing, with unknowns in all positions, e.g., by using objects, drawings, and equations with a symbol for the unknown number to represent the problem.	Unit 1 Lessons 2, 3, 4, 5, 6, 7, 8; Unit 2 Lessons 1, 2, 3, 4, 6, 8, 10, 11, 12, 13, 14, 15, 16; Unit 3 Lessons 2, 3, 4, 5, 6, 7, 8, 9, 10, 11, 12; Unit 4 Lesson 5; Unit 5 Lessons 1, 2, 3, 4, 5, 11; Unit 6 Lessons 1, 2, 3, 4, 5, 6, 7, 8, 9
1.OA.A.2	Solve word problems that call for addition of three whole numbers whose sum is less than or equal to 20, e.g., by using objects, drawings, and equations with a symbol for the unknown number to represent the problem.	Unit 5 Lessons 6, 11; Unit 6 Lessons 1, 4, 5, 9

Understand and apply properties of operations and the relationship between addition and subtraction.

1.OA.B.3	Apply properties of operations as strategies to add and subtract.	Unit 1 Lessons 3, 4, 5, 6, 7, 8, 9; Unit 2 Lessons 7, 8, 9, 13; Unit 3 Lesson 5; Unit 4 Lessons 5, 10; Unit 5 Lessons 4, 6
1.OA.B.4	Understand subtraction as an unknown-addend problem.	Unit 3 Lessons 6, 7, 8, 9, 10, 12; Unit 5 Lessons 2, 5, 10

Add and subtract within 20.

1.OA.C.5	Relate counting to addition and subtraction (e.g., by counting on 2 to add 2).	Unit 1 Lessons 1, 2, 3, 4, 9; Unit 2 Lessons 5, 6, 7, 8, 9; Unit 3 Lessons 1, 3, 4, 6, 7, 11; Unit 4 Lessons 1, 4, 5, 7, 15, 16, 17; Unit 5 Lessons 1, 2, 4

■ **Major**   ■ **Supporting**   ■ **Additional**

1.OA.C.6	Add and subtract within 20, demonstrating fluency for addition and subtraction within 10. Use strategies such as counting on; making ten (e.g., $8 + 6 = 8 + 2 + 4 = 10 + 4 = 14$); decomposing a number leading to a ten (e.g., $13 - 4 = 13 - 3 - 1 = 10 - 1 = 9$); using the relationship between addition and subtraction (e.g., knowing that $8 + 4 = 12$, one knows $12 - 8 = 4$); and creating equivalent but easier or known sums (e.g., adding $6 + 7$ by creating the known equivalent $6 + 6 + 1 = 12 + 1 = 13$).	Unit 1 Lessons 3, 4, 5, 6, 7, 8, 9; Unit 2 Lessons 1, 2, 3, 5, 6, 7, 8, 9, 10, 11, 12, 13, 14, 15, 16; Unit 3 Lessons 1, 3, 4, 5, 6, 7, 10, 11, 12; Unit 4 Lessons 4, 5, 6, 10, 15; Unit 5 Lessons 1, 2, 3, 4, 5, 10, 11; Unit 6 Lessons 3, 8; Unit 7 Lessons 5, 8, 13; Unit 8 Lesson 5

Work with addition and subtraction equations.

1.OA.D.7	Understand the meaning of the equal sign, and determine if equations involving addition and subtraction are true or false.	Unit 2 Lessons 3, 4, 11, 12, 13, 16; Unit 3 Lesson 12; Unit 5 Lesson 11
1.OA.D.8	Determine the unknown whole number in an addition or subtraction equation relating three whole numbers.	Unit 1 Lessons 3, 4, 5, 6, 7, 8; Unit 2 Lessons 5, 6, 7, 8, 9, 10, 12, 13, 14, 16; Unit 3 Lessons 3, 4, 5, 6, 7, 8, 9, 11, 12; Unit 4 Lessons 4, 5, 6, 10, 13, 14, 15, 16; Unit 5 Lessons 1, 2, 3, 4, 5, 10; Unit 6 Lessons 6, 7

1.NBT Number and Operations in Base Ten

Extend the counting sequence.

1.NBT.A.1	Count to 120, starting at any number less than 120. In this range, read and write numerals and represent a number of objects with a written numeral.	Unit 4 Lessons 1, 2, 7, 8, 9, 10, 11, 15, 16, 18; Unit 5 Lessons 7, 8, 9; Unit 6 Lesson 6

■ **Major**   ■ **Supporting**   ☐ **Additional**

Understand place value.

1.NBT.B.2	Understand that the two digits of a two-digit number represent amounts of tens and ones. Understand the following as special cases:	Unit 4 Lessons 1, 2, 3, 4, 7, 8, 9, 10, 11, 12, 13, 14, 16, 17, 18; Unit 5 Lessons 7, 8, 9; Unit 8 Lesson 1
1.NBT.B.2.a	a. 10 can be thought of as a bundle of ten ones — called a "ten."	Unit 4 Lessons 1, 2, 3, 4, 9, 10, 16, 18; Unit 5 Lessons 8, 10; Unit 8 Lesson 1
1.NBT.B.2.b	b. The numbers from 11 to 19 are composed of a ten and one, two, three, four, five, six, seven, eight, or nine ones.	Unit 4 Lessons 2, 3, 4, 5, 8, 10; Unit 5 Lesson 8
1.NBT.B.2.c	c. The numbers 10, 20, 30, 40, 50, 60, 70, 80, 90 refer to one, two, three, four, five, six, seven, eight, or nine tens (and 0 ones).	Unit 4 Lessons 1, 7, 8, 9, 13, 14, 18; Unit 5 Lesson 10; Unit 8 Lesson 1
1.NBT.B.3	Compare two two-digit numbers based on meanings of the tens and ones digits, recording the results of comparisons with the symbols >, =, and <.	Unit 4 Lessons 3, 12, 16, 18; Unit 8 Lesson 6

Use place value understanding and properties of operations to add and subtract.

1.NBT.C.4	Add within 100, including adding a two-digit number and a one-digit number, and adding a two-digit number and a multiple of 10, using concrete models or drawings and strategies based on place value, properties of operations, and/or the relationship between addition and subtraction; relate the strategy to a written method and explain the reasoning used. Understand that in adding two-digit numbers, one adds tens and tens, ones and ones; and sometimes it is necessary to compose a ten.	Unit 4 Lessons 9, 10, 11, 13, 14, 15, 16, 17, 18; Unit 5 Lessons 9, 10, 11; Unit 8 Lessons 1, 2, 3, 4, 5, 6
1.NBT.C.5	Given a two-digit number, mentally find 10 more or 10 less than the number, without having to count; explain the reasoning used.	Unit 5 Lessons 8, 9
1.NBT.C.6	Subtract multiples of 10 in the range 10–90 from multiples of 10 in the range 10–90 (positive or zero differences), using concrete models or drawings and strategies based on place value, properties of operations, and/or the relationship between addition and subtraction; relate the strategy to a written method and explain the reasoning used.	Unit 5 Lessons 9, 10, 11; Unit 8 Lesson 6

1.MD Measurement and Data

Measure lengths indirectly and by iterating length units.

1.MD.A.1	Order three objects by length; compare the lengths of two objects indirectly by using a third object.	Unit 7 Lessons 12, 14
1.MD.A.2	Express the length of an object as a whole number of length units, by laying multiple copies of a shorter object (the length unit) end to end; understand that the length measurement of an object is the number of same-size length units that span it with no gaps or overlaps.	Unit 7 Lessons 13, 14

Tell and write time.

1.MD.B.3	Tell and write time in hours and half-hours using analog and digital clocks.	Unit 7 Lessons 1, 2, 3, 4, 5, 14

Represent and interpret data.

1.MD.C.4	Organize, represent, and interpret data with up to three categories; ask and answer questions about the total number of data points, how many in each category, and how many more or less are in one category than in another.	Unit 6 Lessons 1, 2, 3, 4, 5, 9

1.G Geometry

Reason with shapes and their attributes.

1.G.A.1	Distinguish between defining attributes (e.g., triangles are closed and three-sided) versus non-defining attributes (e.g., color, orientation, overall size); build and draw shapes to possess defining attributes.	Unit 7 Lessons 6, 7, 8, 9, 10
1.G.A.2	Compose two-dimensional shapes (rectangles, squares, trapezoids, triangles, half-circles, and quarter-circles) or three-dimensional shapes (cubes, right rectangular prisms, right circular cones, and right circular cylinders) to create a composite shape, and compose new shapes from the composite shape.	Unit 7 Lessons 9, 10, 11
1.G.A.3	Partition circles and rectangles into two and four equal shares, describe the shares using the words *halves*, *fourths*, and *quarters*, and use the phrases *half of, fourth of,* and *quarter of*. Describe the whole as two of, or four of the shares. Understand for these examples that decomposing into more equal shares creates smaller shares.	Unit 7 Lessons 8, 9, 14

■ **Major** ■ **Supporting** ■ **Additional**

© Houghton Mifflin Harcourt Publishing Company

MP1 Make sense of problems and persevere in solving them.

Mathematically proficient students start by explaining to themselves the meaning of a problem and looking for entry points to its solution. They analyze givens, constraints, relationships, and goals. They make conjectures about the form and meaning of the solution and plan a solution pathway rather than simply jumping into a solution attempt. They consider analogous problems, and try special cases and simpler forms of the original problem in order to gain insight into its solution. They monitor and evaluate their progress and change course if necessary. Older students might, depending on the context of the problem, transform algebraic expressions or change the viewing window on their graphing calculator to get the information they need. Mathematically proficient students can explain correspondences between equations, verbal descriptions, tables, and graphs or draw diagrams of important features and relationships, graph data, and search for regularity or trends. Younger students might rely on using concrete objects or pictures to help conceptualize and solve a problem. Mathematically proficient students check their answers to problems using a different method, and they continually ask themselves, "Does this make sense?" They can understand the approaches of others to solving complex problems and identify correspondences between different approaches.

Unit 1 Lessons 2, 3, 4, 6, 8, 9
Unit 2 Lessons 1, 2, 3, 4, 6, 7, 8, 9, 10, 13, 14, 16
Unit 3 Lessons 1, 2, 3, 4, 6, 7, 8, 9, 10, 11, 12
Unit 4 Lessons 2, 5, 10, 18
Unit 5 Lessons 1, 2, 3, 4, 5, 6, 11
Unit 6 Lessons 1, 2, 4, 6, 7, 8, 9
Unit 7 Lessons 8, 14
Unit 8 Lessons 1, 3, 4, 6

MP2 Reason abstractly and quantitatively.

Mathematically proficient students make sense of quantities and their relationships in problem situations. They bring two complementary abilities to bear on problems involving quantitative relationships: the ability to *decontextualize*—to abstract a given situation and represent it symbolically and manipulate the representing symbols as if they have a life of their own, without necessarily attending to their referents—and the ability to *contextualize*, to pause as needed during the manipulation process in order to probe into the referents for the symbols involved. Quantitative reasoning entails habits of creating a coherent representation of the problem at hand; considering the units involved; attending to the meaning of quantities, not just how to compute them; and knowing and flexibly using different properties of operations and objects.

Unit 1 Lessons 3, 4, 5, 6, 7, 8, 9
Unit 2 Lessons 1, 2, 3, 4, 6, 10, 11, 12, 13, 15, 16
Unit 3 Lessons 3, 5, 6, 12
Unit 4 Lessons 1, 3, 4, 6, 7, 8, 9, 10, 11, 12, 14, 15, 16, 17, 18
Unit 5 Lessons 1, 2, 3, 4, 5, 9, 10, 11
Unit 6 Lessons 1, 2, 3, 5, 6, 8, 9
Unit 7 Lessons 8, 9, 14
Unit 8 Lessons 1, 2, 3, 4, 5, 6

MP3 Construct viable arguments and critique the reasoning of others.

Mathematically proficient students understand and use stated assumptions, definitions, and previously established results in constructing arguments. They make conjectures and build a logical progression of statements to explore the truth of their conjectures. They are able to analyze situations by breaking them into cases, and can recognize and use counterexamples. They justify their conclusions, communicate them to others, and respond to the arguments of others. They reason inductively about data, making plausible arguments that take into account the context from which the data arose. Mathematically proficient students are also able to compare the effectiveness of two plausible arguments, distinguish correct logic or reasoning from that which is flawed, and—if there is a flaw in an argument—explain what it is. Elementary students can construct arguments using concrete referents such as objects, drawings, diagrams, and actions. Such arguments can make sense and be correct, even though they are not generalized or made formal until later grades. Later, students learn to determine domains to which an argument applies. Students at all grades can listen or read the arguments of others, decide whether they make sense, and ask useful questions to clarify or improve the arguments.

Unit 1 Lessons 1, 2, 3, 4, 5, 6, 7, 8, 9
Unit 2 Lessons 1, 2, 3, 4, 6, 7, 8, 9, 10, 11, 12, 13, 14, 16
Unit 3 Lessons 2, 3, 4, 5, 6, 7, 8, 9, 10, 11, 12
Unit 4 Lessons 1, 2, 3, 4, 5, 6, 7, 8, 9, 10, 11, 12, 13, 14, 15, 16, 17, 18
Unit 5 Lessons 1, 2, 3, 4, 5, 6, 7, 8, 9, 10, 11
Unit 6 Lessons 1, 2, 3, 4, 5, 6, 7, 8, 9
Unit 7 Lessons 1, 2, 3, 4, 5, 6, 7, 8, 9, 10, 11, 12, 13, 14
Unit 8 Lessons 1, 2, 3, 4, 5, 6

MP4 Model with mathematics.

Mathematically proficient students can apply the mathematics they know to solve problems arising in everyday life, society, and the workplace. In early grades, this might be as simple as writing an addition equation to describe a situation. In middle grades, a student might apply proportional reasoning to plan a school event or analyze a problem in the community. By high school, a student might use geometry to solve a design problem or use a function to describe how one quantity of interest depends on another. Mathematically proficient students who can apply what they know are comfortable making assumptions and approximations to simplify a complicated situation, realizing that these may need revision later. They are able to identify important quantities in a practical situation and map their relationships using such tools as diagrams, two-way tables, graphs, flowcharts and formulas. They can analyze those relationships mathematically to draw conclusions. They routinely interpret their mathematical results in the context of the situation and reflect on whether the results make sense, possibly improving the model if it has not served its purpose.

Unit 1 Lessons 2, 3, 9
Unit 2 Lessons 1, 2, 10, 13, 16
Unit 3 Lessons 1, 2, 5, 6, 7, 8, 9, 10, 11, 12
Unit 4 Lessons 2, 3, 5, 10, 18
Unit 5 Lessons 1, 2, 3, 4, 6, 11
Unit 6 Lessons 2, 3, 4, 5, 6, 7, 8, 9
Unit 7 Lessons 3, 8, 14
Unit 8 Lessons 1, 2, 3, 6

MP5 Use appropriate tools strategically.

Mathematically proficient students consider the available tools when solving a mathematical problem. These tools might include pencil and paper, concrete models, a ruler, a protractor, a calculator, a spreadsheet, a computer algebra system, a statistical package, or dynamic geometry software. Proficient students are sufficiently familiar with tools appropriate for their grade or course to make sound decisions about when each of these tools might be helpful, recognizing both the insight to be gained and their limitations. For example, mathematically proficient high school students analyze graphs of functions and solutions generated using a graphing calculator. They detect possible errors by strategically using estimation and other mathematical knowledge. When making mathematical models, they know that technology can enable them to visualize the results of varying assumptions, explore consequences, and compare predictions with data. Mathematically proficient students at various grade levels are able to identify relevant external mathematical resources, such as digital content located on a website, and use them to pose or solve problems. They are able to use technological tools to explore and deepen their understanding of concepts.

Unit 1 Lessons 1, 2, 3, 4, 5, 6, 7, 8, 9
Unit 2 Lessons 5, 6, 8, 16
Unit 3 Lessons 1, 2, 3, 4, 7, 11, 12
Unit 4 Lessons 1, 2, 3, 4, 5, 6, 7, 8, 9, 10, 11, 12, 13, 14, 16, 17, 18
Unit 5 Lessons 1, 2, 6, 8, 9, 10, 11
Unit 6 Lessons 3, 4, 5, 9
Unit 7 Lessons 1, 2, 5, 6, 7, 8, 9, 10, 11, 12, 13, 14
Unit 8 Lessons 2, 3, 6

MP6 Attend to precision.

Mathematically proficient students try to communicate precisely to others. They try to use clear definitions in discussion with others and in their own reasoning. They state the meaning of the symbols they choose, including using the equal sign consistently and appropriately. They are careful about specifying units of measure, and labeling axes to clarify the correspondence with quantities in a problem. They calculate accurately and efficiently, express numerical answers with a degree of precision appropriate for the problem context. In the elementary grades, students give carefully formulated explanations to each other. By the time they reach high school they have learned to examine claims and make explicit use of definitions.

Unit 1 Lessons 1, 2, 3, 4, 5, 6, 7, 8, 9
Unit 2 Lessons 1, 3, 4, 5, 6, 7, 8, 9, 10, 11, 12, 13, 14, 15, 16
Unit 3 Lessons 1, 2, 3, 4, 5, 6, 7, 8, 9, 10, 11, 12
Unit 4 Lessons 1, 2, 3, 4, 5, 6, 7, 8, 9, 10, 11, 12, 13, 14, 15, 16, 17, 18
Unit 5 Lessons 1, 2, 3, 4, 5, 6, 7, 8, 9, 10, 11
Unit 6 Lessons 1, 2, 3, 4, 5, 6, 7, 8, 9
Unit 7 Lessons 1, 2, 3, 4, 5, 6, 7, 8, 9, 10, 11, 12, 13, 14
Unit 8 Lessons 1, 2, 3, 4, 5, 6

Common Core State Standards for Mathematical Practice

MP7 Look for and make use of structure.

Mathematically proficient students look closely to discern a pattern or structure. Young students, for example, might notice that three and seven more is the same amount as seven and three more, or they may sort a collection of shapes according to how many sides the shapes have. Later, students will see 7×8 equals the well remembered $7 \times 5 + 7 \times 3$, in preparation for learning about the distributive property. In the expression $x^2 + 9x + 14$, older students can see the 14 as 2×7 and the 9 as $2 + 7$. They recognize the significance of an existing line in a geometric figure and can use the strategy of drawing an auxiliary line for solving problems. They also can step back for an overview and shift perspective. They can see complicated things, such as some algebraic expressions, as single objects or as being composed of several objects. For example, they can see $5 - 3(x - y)^2$ as 5 minus a positive number times a square and use that to realize that its value cannot be more than 5 for any real numbers x and y.

Unit 1 Lessons 1, 2, 3, 4, 5, 6, 7, 8, 9
Unit 2 Lessons 13, 14, 16
Unit 3 Lessons 1, 3, 9, 12
Unit 4 Lessons 1, 2, 3, 5, 6, 7, 8, 9, 10,13, 17, 18
Unit 5 Lessons 1, 2, 3, 5, 6, 7, 8, 9, 10, 11
Unit 6 Lessons 6, 8, 9
Unit 7 Lessons 1, 2, 3, 4, 5, 6, 7, 9, 10, 11, 14
Unit 8 Lessons 2, 6

MP8 Look for and express regularity in repeated reasoning.

Mathematically proficient students notice if calculations are repeated, and look both for general methods and for shortcuts. Upper elementary students might notice when dividing 25 by 11 that they are repeating the same calculations over and over again, and conclude they have a repeating decimal. By paying attention to the calculation of slope as they repeatedly check whether points are on the line through (1, 2) with slope 3, middle school students might abstract the equation $(y - 2)/(x - 1) = 3$. Noticing the regularity in the way terms cancel when expanding $(x - 1)(x + 1)$, $(x - 1)(x^2 + x + 1)$, and $(x - 1)(x^3 + x^2 + x + 1)$ might lead them to the general formula for the sum of a geometric series. As they work to solve a problem, mathematically proficient students maintain oversight of the process, while attending to the details. They continually evaluate the reasonableness of their intermediate results.

Unit 1 Lessons 1, 2, 3, 4, 5, 6, 7, 8, 9
Unit 2 Lessons 6, 7, 8, 11, 14, 16
Unit 3 Lessons 8, 9, 12
Unit 4 Lessons 1, 2, 5, 6, 7, 9, 10, 12, 13, 14, 15, 17, 18
Unit 5 Lessons 1, 2, 4, 5, 6, 7, 8, 9, 10, 11
Unit 6 Lessons 1, 6, 7, 9
Unit 7 Lessons 3, 6, 7, 8, 9, 10, 12, 14
Unit 8 Lessons 1, 2, 3, 4, 6

Index

Commutative Property, 23, 25, 27, 29

Zero Property, 20, 22, 26, 30

situation and solution equations, 123–124, 263

symbols

equal (=), 47–48, 152, 188

inequality (<, >), 177–178, 188

minus (–), 71–78

plus (+), 15–16, 43–44

unknown addends, 97–102, 107–108, 124, 154, 207–208, 215

writing an equation, 47–48, 73–76, 109, 117, 133–134, 159, 220

writing a related equation, 81–82, 123–124, 263

Assessment

Fluency Check, 52, 70, 80, 88, 112, 122, 136, 164, 180, 194, 224, 238, 260, 270, 296, 318, 326, 348

Formative Assessment

Performance Task, 38–39, 93–94, 141–142, 199–200, 243–244, 275–276, 331–332, 353–354

Unit Review/Test, 34–37, 89–92, 137–140, 195–198, 239–242, 271–274, 327–330, 349–352

Quick Quiz, 13, 33, 51, 69, 79, 87, 111, 121, 135, 163, 179, 193, 223, 237, 259, 269, 295, 317, 325, 347

Strategy Check, 14, 34

Attributes. *See* **Geometry; Sorting and classifying.**

B

Break-aparts

Break-Apart Stick, 15, 17, 19, 21

C

Circle, 303–304

Circle drawings, 21, 23, 27, 29, 45–49, 73–77, 123–124, 151–152

Clock. *See also* **Time.**

analog, 281–282, 287–295

digital, 282, 291–292, 293–294

hour hand, 282–283, 285–286, 291–294

minute hand, 282–283, 291–294

for "Our Busy Day" Book, 287–288

Columns, 229–231

Common Core Standards, S17–S24

Commutative Property, 23. *See also* **Addition.**

Compare. *See* **Length; Numbers.**

Comparison bars, 261–266

Cone, 313–314, 315–316

Corners, 301, 303–304, 310

Counting

to 10, 31

count on, 55–60, 68–69, 101, 188

One Hundred Twenty Grid, 229–231

number words, 167–168

read and write numerals, 31, 167–168, 189–190, 229–230

represent a set with a written numeral, 43–44, 145, 148, 249–250

represent a set with drawings, 249–252

tens and ones, 145–148, 165–166, 168, 189–190, 225–226

Cube, 313–314, 315–316

Cylinder, 313–314, 315–316

Index

Problem solving. *See* Addition; Problem Types; Subtraction.

Problem Types, S1–S3

Add To with Change Unknown, 97–102, 107–108, 119–120, 123–124, 125–126, 131, 208, 219

Add To with Result Unknown, 81, 124–126

Add To with Start Unknown, 125–126, 127–128, 208, 219, 236

Compare with Bigger Unknown, 263, 265–266

Compare with Difference Unknown, 261–262, 264, 265–266, 268

Compare with Smaller Unknown, 263–264, 265–266, 268

Put Together/Take Apart with Addend Unknown, 97–102, 107–108, 119–120, 123–124, 208, 215

Put Together/Take Apart with Both Addends Unknown, 100, 215

Put Together/Take Apart with Total Unknown, 81, 85, 128, 208, 219–220, 216

Take From with Change Unknown, 125, 128, 216

Take From with Result Unknown, 81, 107–108, 119, 128, 216

Take From with Start Unknown, 124, 128, 131, 216, 220, 236

Properties

Associative (addition), 221–222, 235–236, 337–338

Commutative (addition), 23, 25, 27

Zero (addition), 20, 22, 26, 30

Puzzled Penguin, 72, 102, 153, 178, 184, 220, 234, 253, 286, 292, 344

Q

Quick Quiz, 13, 33, 51, 69, 79, 87, 111, 121, 135, 163, 179, 193, 223, 237, 259, 269, 295, 317, 325, 347

R

Real world problems. *See* Problem Types.

Rectangle, 301–302

Rectangular prism, 313–314, 315–316

Rows, 229–231

S

Show All Totals Method, 341

Sides, 301, 303–304

Sorting and classifying

by attribute, 301, 314

by category, 247, 249–255

by shape, 302

Sphere, 313–314, 315

Square, 301

Strategy Check, 14, 34

Student Clock, 283–284

Subtraction

within 10, 30, 71–78, 81–82, 83–86, 107–108, 117–120, 124–128, 133–134

within 20, 213–214, 215–216, 217–218, 219–220, 236

determine the unknown whole number, 113, 119, 124–128, 132–133, 215–216, 220, 235–236

equation, 71–78, 213–214

T

New Group Below method, 337–343

Show All Totals method, 341

add with properties, 337–338

compose a ten, 185, 188, 335–336, 337–343, 345–346, 347, 349–352

counting on, 185, 188

relate addition and subtraction, 232

of tens, 229–232

add with concrete models, 191–192

subtraction

relate addition and subtraction, 232

subtract with models, 236

subtract with place value, 236

of tens, 229–230, 232

Two-dimensional shapes. *See* **Geometry; Manipulatives.**

Two-Dimensional Shape Set, 297–300, 312

Illustrator: Josh Brill

Did you ever try to use shapes to draw animals like the frog on the cover?

Over the last 10 years Josh has been using geometric shapes to design his animals. His aim is to keep the animal drawings simple and use color to make them appealing.

Add some color to the frog Josh drew. Then try drawing a cat or dog or some other animal using the shapes below.

Shape Toolbox